The Holy Spirit
The Teacher of All Truth

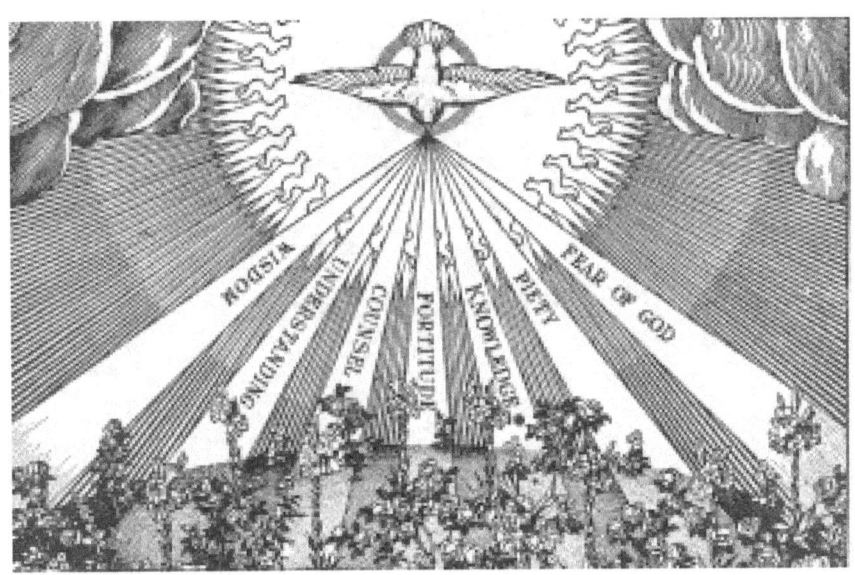

Karajah Yashar

Orlando, FL

www.bspbooks.com

ISBN: 978-1-962691-39-0

First Edition: August 2024

Table of Contents

Chapter 1: Origins of the Holy Spirit........4

Chapter 2: The Holy Spirit Defined.........9

Chapter 3: Steps to Receive the Holy Spirit....................................20

Chapter 4: The Holy Spirit in the Life of Disciples..................................30

Chapter 5: Fruits of the Spirit...............38

Chapter 6: Eliminating False Gods........54

Chapter 7: Teaching All Truth................59

Chapter 8: Conviction of Sin.................71

Chapter 9: Spiritual Warfare.................75

Chapter 10: The Gifts of the Holy Spirit....92

Chapter 11: The Role of the Holy Spirit in Prayer and Intercession......................111

Chapter 12: Walking in the Spirit.........118

About the Author.................................125

Chapter 1: Origins of the Holy Spirit

The Holy Spirit, often associated with the New Testament and the Day of Pentecost, is deeply rooted in the entire Biblical narrative, including the Old Testament. While the full revelation of the Holy Spirit's role comes into sharper focus in the New Testament, His presence and work are evident throughout the Old Testament. From the act of creation to the empowerment of leaders and prophets, the Holy Spirit's activity in the Old Testament lays the foundation for understanding His ongoing work in the world.

The Holy Spirit in Creation

The very first chapter of the Bible introduces the Holy Spirit as an active participant in the creation of the universe. Genesis 1:2 states, "And the earth was without form, and void; and darkness was upon the face of the deep. And the Spirit of God moved upon the face of the waters." Here, the "Spirit of God" is depicted as hovering over the primordial waters, bringing order out of chaos and life out of nothingness. This imagery conveys the Holy Spirit's role as a life-giver and sustainer, integral to the creative work of God.

The Spirit's involvement in creation underscores His power, creativity, and authority, setting the stage for His continued activity throughout the Biblical narrative.

Empowerment of Leaders

The Holy Spirit's presence in the Old Testament is also evident in His empowerment of leaders chosen by God for specific tasks. One of the most prominent examples is the anointing of Moses and the seventy elders to lead the Israelites. In Numbers 11:25, we read, "And the Lord came down in a cloud, and spake unto him, and took of the spirit that was upon him, and gave it unto the seventy elders: and it came to pass, that, when the spirit rested upon them, they prophesied, and did not cease." The Holy Spirit enabled these leaders to carry out their divine mission with wisdom, strength, and prophetic insight. Similarly, the judges, kings, and prophets of Israel often received the Spirit's anointing to fulfill their God-given roles. For instance, in 1 Samuel 16:13, "the Spirit of the Lord came upon David from that day forward," equipping him to lead Israel as king.

The Prophets and the Spirit

The Holy Spirit's work is perhaps most vividly seen in the ministry of the prophets. The prophets were God's messengers, often delivering challenging and convicting words to the people of Israel. The Holy Spirit inspired and guided these prophets, enabling them to speak God's truth with authority and power. Isaiah 61:1 famously declares, "The Spirit of the Lord God is upon me; because the Lord hath anointed me to preach good tidings unto the meek; he hath sent me to bind up the brokenhearted, to proclaim liberty to the captives, and the opening of the prison to them that are bound." This verse, later quoted by Jesus in the New Testament, illustrates the Spirit's role in empowering the prophets to proclaim God's message and bring hope to His people.

The Promise of the Spirit's Future Work

The Old Testament also anticipates the future outpouring of the Holy Spirit, which would be realized in the New Testament. The prophet Joel, under the inspiration of the Holy Spirit, foretold a time when the Spirit would be poured out on all people, not just a select few. Joel 2:28 prophesies, "And it shall come to pass afterward, that I will pour out my spirit upon all flesh; and your sons and your daughters shall prophesy, your old men shall dream dreams, your young men shall see visions." This promise looked forward to the Day of Pentecost, where the Holy Spirit would be given to all disciples, marking the beginning of a new era in God's relationship with humanity.

Weaving the Old and New Testament

The Holy Spirit's presence in the Old Testament is a testament to His eternal nature and active involvement in God's plan for creation and redemption. From the dawn of creation to the anointing of leaders and the inspiration of prophets, the Holy Spirit was at work, guiding, empowering, and sustaining God's people. Understanding the Holy Spirit's role in the Old Testament enriches our comprehension of His work in the New Testament and in our lives today. As we trace the Holy Spirit's presence through the pages of Scripture, we see a consistent thread of divine activity, culminating in the outpouring of the Spirit on all disciples, as foretold by the prophets of old.

immanent aspects. Economically, the Holy Spirit operates in the world, fulfilling God's redemptive plan. The Holy Spirit empowered Jesus during His ministry (Luke 4:18), inspired the apostles, and continues to work in the Church today. Immanently, the Holy Spirit exists in a perfect and eternal relationship with the Father and the Son, sharing in the divine essence and eternal love that characterizes the Godhead.

Chapter 2: The Holy Spirit Defined

The Holy Spirit, often referred to as the Most High God manifest, embodies the active presence and power of God in the world. Just as God the Father is the "I Am," the eternal and self-existent One, the Holy Spirit represents His dynamic involvement in creation, sustaining life, guiding humanity, and fulfilling divine purposes. In a way similar to how our own words, actions, and influence are extensions of who we are, the Holy Spirit is the extension of God's essence, manifesting His will and character throughout the universe.

When we consider our own lives, we see that we are more than just physical beings; we are defined by our actions, the impact we have on others, and the presence we carry. These are expressions of our spirit. Similarly, God the Father's works in the universe and through people, as well as His communication through anointed individuals, are the manifestations of His Holy Spirit. The Spirit is God's way of being intimately involved in His creation, moving in the hearts of people, and bringing about His purposes on earth. It is through the Holy Spirit that God's presence is made known and felt, guiding, convicting, and empowering those who seek Him.

Jesus, as the love of God manifest in flesh, represents the ultimate expression of God's creative and redemptive love. Just as a child is a tangible manifestation of a parent's love, Jesus is the tangible manifestation of God's love for humanity. The Holy Spirit and Jesus are distinct yet united in expressing the fullness of God. While Jesus walked the earth as God's son incarnate, the Holy Spirit is the work of God, dwelling within disciples and enabling them to live out God's will. Together, they reveal the depth and breadth of God's character—God the Father as the "I Am," Jesus as His love made flesh, and the Holy Spirit as His active presence and power in the world.

Attributes of the Holy Spirit

The Holy Spirit has the essential attributes of God. These attributes include:

Eternality: The Holy Spirit is often referred to as the "eternal Spirit". Hebrews 9:14 speaks to this eternal aspect, stating, "How much more shall the blood of Christ, who through the eternal Spirit offered himself without spot to God, purge your conscience from dead works to serve the living God?" This verse highlights that the Holy Spirit, like the Father and the Son, exists beyond the constraints of time, having neither beginning nor end. This eternal nature underscores the Holy Spirit's divine nature and affirms its presence throughout all of history, from the creation of the world to the consummation of God's plan for humanity.

The concept of eternality aligns the Holy Spirit with the eternal nature of God the Father and Jesus Christ. Just as God is described as the "Alpha and Omega, the beginning and the end" (Revelation 22:13), His Holy Spirit is equally timeless, participating in the divine will across all ages. This eternal existence of the Holy Spirit means that its presence and influence have always been and will always be active in the world, guiding, comforting, and empowering disciples. The Holy Spirit's timelessness is a reminder of God's unchanging nature and His everlasting commitment to His creation.

Understanding the Holy Spirit's eternality also deepens our appreciation for the unbroken continuity of God's work in the world. From the inspiration of the prophets in the Old Testament to the indwelling of disciples in the New Testament, the Holy Spirit's presence spans the entire Biblical narrative, demonstrating its ongoing involvement as God's redemptive plan. This eternal presence assures disciples that the Holy Spirit, as the mind and breath of the eternal God, is always with us, guiding us in truth and sustaining our faith until the end of time.

Omnipresence: The Holy Spirit's omnipresence is a profound aspect of His divine nature, affirming that He is present everywhere at all times. Psalm 139:7-10 captures the essence of this truth, asking, "Whither shall I go from thy spirit? or whither shall I flee from thy presence? If I ascend up into heaven, thou art there: if I make my bed in hell, behold, thou art there. If I take the wings of the morning, and dwell in the uttermost parts of the sea; even there shall thy hand lead me, and thy right hand shall hold me." These verses poetically express the reality that there is no place in the universe where the Spirit of God is absent, highlighting the comforting truth that God is always near.

The omnipresence of the Holy Spirit assures disciples that they are never alone. Whether in times of joy or sorrow, triumph or trial, the Holy Spirit is constantly with them, providing guidance, comfort, and strength. This constant presence is a source of profound peace for disciples, knowing that the Spirit is with them wherever they go and in whatever circumstances they find themselves. It is through the Holy Spirit that God fulfills His promise to never leave nor forsake His people, making His presence felt in every moment of their lives.

Moreover, the Holy Spirit's omnipresence emphasizes His active role in the life of every disciple, regardless of location or situation. This means that disciples can experience the Spirit's influence whether they are alone in prayer, gathered in worship, or engaged in the ordinary tasks of life. The Spirit's omnipresence breaks down barriers of time and space, uniting disciples in a shared experience of God's love and power. This universal presence of the Holy Spirit is a testament to His divine nature and an essential aspect of His work in the world, continually drawing people closer to God and empowering them to live out their faith.

Omniscience: The Holy Spirit's omniscience, or all-knowing nature, is a key aspect of the Spirit of God, affirming that He possesses complete and perfect knowledge. In 1 Corinthians 2:10-11, Paul writes, "But God hath revealed them unto us by his Spirit: for the Spirit searcheth all things, yea, the deep things of God. For what man knoweth the things of a man, save the spirit of man which is in him? even so the things of God knoweth no man, but the Spirit of God." This passage highlights the Holy Spirit's ability to search and understand even the most profound and hidden aspects of God's will and character. The Spirit's omniscience ensures that God is fully aware of everything in creation and beyond, from the grandest cosmic events to the deepest thoughts and intentions of the human heart.

The Holy Spirit's perfect knowledge also makes it the ultimate teacher and guide for disciples. Jesus promised that the Holy Spirit would "teach you all things, and bring all things to your remembrance, whatsoever I have said unto you" (John 14:26). This promise reveals the Spirit's role in illuminating the truths of Scripture, helping disciples to understand and apply God's Word in their lives. The Holy Spirit's omniscience allows Him to instruct and remind disciples in a way that is perfectly suited to their individual needs, guiding them in truth and helping them to grow in their relationship with God. His knowledge is not just intellectual but deeply personal, providing wisdom and insight that leads to spiritual growth and transformation.

Furthermore, the Holy Spirit's omniscience is a source of great comfort and assurance for disciples. Knowing that the Holy Spirit possesses complete understanding of all things, including the future, disciples can trust in His guidance and leading, even when circumstances are uncertain or challenging. The Spirit's knowledge encompasses not only the mysteries of God but also the details of each disciple's life, enabling Him to provide exactly what is needed at the right time. This profound knowledge assures disciples that they are never alone in their journey of faith, as the Holy Spirit continually works to reveal God's will and purpose, guiding them toward a deeper understanding and a closer walk with their Creator.

Omnipotence: The Holy Spirit's omnipotence, or unlimited power, is a defining attribute of its divine nature, manifesting throughout Scripture in both the physical and spiritual realms. From the very beginning, the Spirit's power is evident in the creation of the world, as Genesis 1:2 describes, "And the Spirit of God moved upon the face of the waters." This powerful act of creation shows the Holy Spirit's role in bringing order and life into existence, emphasizing that its power is not only vast but foundational to the existence of all things.

The Holy Spirit's power is further demonstrated in the resurrection of Jesus Christ, one of the most significant events ever. Romans 8:11 states, "But if the Spirit of him that raised up Jesus from the dead dwell in you, he that raised up Christ from the dead shall also quicken your mortal bodies by his Spirit that dwelleth in you." This verse highlights the Holy Spirit's role in bringing Jesus back to life, showcasing His power over death itself. The resurrection is not only a demonstration of the Spirit's omnipotence but also a promise of the same power at work within disciples, offering the hope of eternal life and transformation through the Spirit's indwelling presence.

Beyond these grand acts, the Holy Spirit's omnipotence is continually at work in the lives of disciples, transforming hearts and minds to reflect the character of Christ. This transformative power is seen in the process of sanctification, where the Holy Spirit empowers disciples to overcome sin, grow in holiness, and live according to God's will. The Spirit's omnipotence ensures that no challenge or obstacle is too great for God's intervention, whether it be in the physical world or in the inner spiritual life of a person. This active and dynamic presence of the Holy Spirit reinforces the role of the all-powerful God, intimately involved in the ongoing work of redemption and renewal, guiding and sustaining disciples in their journey of faith.

The Trinity Deception

The concept of the Trinity, which describes God as three coequal and coeternal persons—Father, Son, and Holy Spirit—was a doctrine formalized at the Council of Nicaea in 325. This doctrine, while widely accepted in many Christian traditions, is not found in the Bible. The Scripture consistently portrays God as One, with the Holy Spirit being the Spirit of God and Jesus as His Son, distinct in role and nature but not equal in essence to God the Father. Key verses such as Deuteronomy 6:4, "Hear, O Israel: The Lord our God is one Lord," emphasize the oneness of God, challenging the notion of a coequal Trinity.

In the New Testament, Jesus Himself consistently acknowledges the Father's greater authority and never claims to be equal with God. In John 14:28, Jesus says, "My Father is greater than I," which is a clear indication of the distinct roles and hierarchy within the relationship between God the Father and Jesus. Furthermore, Jesus prays to the Father, seeks His will, and submits to His authority, all of which suggest a relationship that is not one of coequality but of divine Sonship and servitude. This relationship aligns more closely with the view that Jesus, while divinely appointed, operates under the authority of God the Father, rather than being His equal. Jesus emphatically states "Why callest thou me good? there is none good but one, that is, God: but if thou wilt enter into life, keep the commandments" Mathew 19:17.

The Holy Spirit, according to this perspective, is understood not as a separate person but as the presence and power of God at work in the world. Verses like Acts 2:17, where God says, "I will pour out my Spirit upon all flesh," indicate that the Holy Spirit is an extension of God's being, not a distinct entity. This understanding preserves the unity and singularity of God, emphasizing His oneness rather than dividing His essence into three separate persons. The true Biblical teaching is that God is One, with Jesus as His Son and the Holy Spirit as His divine presence and power.

Chapter 3: Steps to Receive the Holy Spirit

Receiving the Holy Spirit is a significant and transformative experience in the life of a disciple. It marks the beginning of a deep and ongoing relationship with God, empowering the individual to live out their faith and fulfill their divine calling. The process of receiving the Holy Spirit is rooted in several key steps, each of which is crucial for preparing the heart and mind to welcome this divine presence. These steps— A clean heart, faith in Jesus Christ, repentance, baptism, prayer and laying on of hands, and obedience and surrender—are foundational to the Disciple's journey and provide a pathway for receiving the Holy Spirit.

A Clean Heart

God, in His sovereignty and infinite wisdom, imparts the Holy Spirit upon those whom He deems worthy according to His divine will and purpose. This act is not based on human merit or achievements but on God's grace and the condition of the heart. Scripture shows that God knows the hearts of individuals and grants the Holy Spirit to those who are genuinely seeking

Him, repentant, and obedient to His will. The Apostle Peter acknowledged this when he said, "God, who knows the heart, showed that he accepted them by giving the Holy Spirit to them" (Acts 15:8). God's impartation of the Holy Spirit is an expression of His love and desire for disciple s to be empowered, guided, and transformed in their spiritual journey. It is a gift that aligns with His eternal plan, given freely to those who are open and ready to receive it, according to His perfect judgment.

God's impartation of the Holy Spirit to those with a pure heart and a sincere pursuit of righteousness is a testament to His desire for intimate and transformative relationships with His followers. A pure heart, one that is free from deceit, malice, and selfish intentions, is a vessel ready to be filled with the Holy Spirit. Jesus Himself emphasized the importance of inner purity, stating, "Blessed are the pure in heart, for they shall see God" (Matthew 5:8). This purity of heart reflects a deep longing to align one's life with God's will, seeking not only to follow His commandments but also to embody His love, justice, and mercy in all aspects of life. Such individuals, motivated by a genuine love for God and a commitment to righteousness, are prime candidates for the Holy Spirit's indwelling presence.

In their pursuit of righteousness, these disciple s demonstrate a sincere desire to live in accordance with God's standards, striving to reflect His character in their daily lives. This pursuit is not about self-righteousness or legalistic adherence to rules but about a heartfelt commitment to God's ways. Scripture reveals that God is drawn to those who hunger and thirst for righteousness, promising that they will be filled (Matthew 5:6). The filling of the Holy Spirit is God's response to this deep spiritual longing, equipping disciple s with the strength, wisdom, and guidance needed to live out their faith authentically. Through the Holy Spirit, God empowers them to resist temptation, overcome sin, and grow in holiness, making them increasingly conformed to the image of Christ.

God's willingness to impart the Holy Spirit to those who have a pure heart and seek righteousness also reflects His grace and desire for partnership with humanity. He delights in those who earnestly seek Him and rewards their devotion by granting them His Spirit, enabling them to fulfill their divine calling. This impartation is a sacred trust, as the Holy Spirit not only comforts and guides but also convicts and challenges disciple s to continue their pursuit of purity and righteousness. It is through the Holy Spirit that they are transformed from the inside out, becoming vessels of God's love and power in the world. This divine partnership illustrates the profound truth that God does not just call His followers to righteousness; He equips them for it, pouring out His Spirit on those whose hearts are fully committed to Him.

Faith in Jesus Christ

An essential step in receiving the Holy Spirit is becoming open too and obedient too Jesus Christ. This faith is not merely intellectual assent but involves a deep, personal commitment to Jesus as Lord and Savior. When an individual believes in Jesus, they acknowledge His sacrifice on the cross for the forgiveness of sins and recognize Him as the only way to salvation. This act of faith is transformative, leading to a new birth, as described by Jesus in His conversation with Nicodemus: "Truly, truly, I say to you, unless one is born of water and the Spirit, he cannot enter the kingdom of God" (John 3:5-8). This new birth signifies the beginning of a spiritual life in which the Holy Spirit comes to dwell within the disciple, guiding, teaching, and empowering them in their walk with God.

Faith in Jesus Christ also involves a commitment to obey His commandments. Jesus Himself emphasized the importance of obedience, stating, "If you love me, you will keep my commandments" (John 14:15). This obedience is not a means of earning the Holy Spirit but is a natural response to the grace and love that God has shown through Jesus. When a disciple truly commits to following Jesus, their life begins to align with God's will, creating an environment in which the Holy Spirit can thrive and work effectively. This step of faith and obedience lays the foundation for all subsequent steps in receiving the Holy Spirit.

Repentance

Repentance is the next crucial step in the process of receiving the Holy Spirit. It involves a conscious decision to turn away from sin and turn toward God, embracing His ways and His will. Sin, as defined in Scripture, is the transgression of God's laws (1 John 3:4). Repentance, therefore, is an acknowledgment of one's sins and a heartfelt desire to be cleansed and forgiven. This turning away from sin is not merely an outward act but involves a deep inward change—a change of heart and mind that results in a transformed life.

Peter, in his sermon on the day of Pentecost, emphasized the necessity of repentance as a prerequisite for receiving the Holy Spirit. He declared, "Repent and be baptized, every one of you, in the name of Jesus Christ for the forgiveness of your sins. And you will receive the gift of the Holy Spirit" (Acts 2:38). This message underscores the importance of repentance in preparing the heart to receive the Holy Spirit. Without repentance, the heart remains closed to God's presence, and the barriers of sin hinder the work of the Holy Spirit. However, when a disciple repents, those barriers are removed, and the way is opened for the Holy Spirit to enter and begin His transformative work.

Baptism

Baptism, while not an absolute requirement for receiving the Holy Spirit, is often closely associated with it in Scripture. Baptism symbolizes the washing away of sins and the disciple's identification with the death, burial, and resurrection of Jesus Christ. It is a public declaration of faith and a step of obedience that signifies the disciple's new life in Christ. In many instances in the New Testament, the reception of the Holy Spirit is linked with the act of baptism. For example, in Acts 19:1-6, Paul encounters a group of disciples who had been baptized with John's baptism of repentance but had not yet received the Holy Spirit. After baptizing them in the name of Jesus, Paul lays hands on them, and they receive the Holy Spirit. However, it is important to note that baptism is not always by water. The Bible also speaks of being baptized by the Spirit. John the Baptist foretold this when he said, "I baptize you with water for repentance. But after me comes one who is more powerful than I, whose sandals I am not worthy to carry. He will baptize you with the Holy Spirit and fire" (Matthew 3:11). This baptism by the Spirit refers to the Holy Spirit's powerful and transformative work in the disciple's life, marking them as God's own and empowering them for His service. Whether by water or by the Spirit, baptism is a significant step in the process of receiving the Holy Spirit, symbolizing the disciple's purification and readiness to receive God's presence.

Prayer and Laying on of Hands

In many accounts in the Book of Acts, the reception of the Holy Spirit is accompanied by prayer and the laying on of hands by other disciples. This practice reflects the early Church's recognition of the importance of community and the role of mature disciples in helping new converts receive the Holy Spirit. For instance, in Acts 8:17, Peter and John pray for the new disciples in Samaria and lay their hands on them, and they receive the Holy Spirit. Similarly, in Acts 19:6, Paul lays hands on the Ephesian disciples, and they too receive the Holy Spirit.

The laying on of hands does not always have to be literal. In Scripture, "hands" often symbolize works or deeds. Thus, following in the works of seasoned disciples—learning from their example, receiving their guidance, and participating in the community of faith—can also be seen as a form of laying on of hands. Through prayer and active engagement in the life of the Church, disciples open themselves to the influence and guidance of the Holy Spirit. This communal aspect of receiving the Holy Spirit emphasizes the importance of fellowship and the shared journey of faith within the body of Christ.

Obedience and Surrender

The final step in receiving the Holy Spirit is a heart that is open, obedient, and surrendered to God's will. Jesus promised that the Father would give the Holy Spirit to those who ask Him, saying, "How much more will your Father in heaven give the Holy Spirit to those who ask Him!" (Luke 11:13). This promise highlights the importance of seeking God earnestly and being receptive to His Spirit. An obedient and surrendered heart is one that is fully aligned with God's purposes, willing to follow wherever He leads.

Obedience involves not just hearing God's word but actively living it out. James 1:22 reminds disciples to "be doers of the word, and not hearers only, deceiving yourselves." When a disciple lives in obedience to God's commands, they create an environment where the Holy Spirit can dwell and work powerfully. Surrender, on the other hand, involves relinquishing control and allowing God to lead. It is an acknowledgment that God's ways are higher than our ways and that His plans are perfect. When a disciple surrenders their will to God, they invite the Holy Spirit to take the lead in their life, guiding, empowering, and transforming them into the likeness of Christ.

In conclusion, receiving the Holy Spirit is a profound and life-changing experience that involves a series of intentional steps. Faith in Jesus Christ, repentance, baptism, prayer, and laying on of hands, along with obedience and surrender, all play crucial roles in preparing the heart and mind to receive this divine gift. As disciples walk through these steps, they open themselves to the powerful and transformative presence of the Holy Spirit, who comes to dwell within them, guiding, teaching, and empowering them for a life of faithful service to God. Through the Holy Spirit, disciples are equipped to fulfill their divine calling and to live out their faith in a way that glorifies God and advances His kingdom on earth.

Chapter 4: The Holy Spirit in the Life of Disciples

The Holy Spirit's presence and activity in the lives of disciples is a testament to His divine nature and loving purpose. Upon accepting and following the commandments of Jesus Christ, disciples receive the Holy Spirit, who indwells them, transforming their hearts and minds. This indwelling presence signifies the intimate and ongoing relationship between God and His people.

Sanctification: The Holy Spirit is central to the process of sanctification, guiding disciples in their spiritual growth and helping them to become more like Christ. Sanctification is the ongoing work of the Holy Spirit in a disciple's life, transforming them from the inside out, renewing their minds, and aligning their desires with God's will. As disciples submit to the Holy Spirit's leading, they experience a deepening of their relationship with God and a progressive growth in holiness. This transformation is not merely about external behaviors but involves a profound change in the heart and mind, enabling disciples to live in a way that honors God.

One of the most tangible types of evidence of the Holy Spirit's work in sanctification is the production of spiritual fruit, as outlined in Galatians 5:22-23. These fruits—love, joy, peace, patience, kindness, goodness, faithfulness, gentleness, and self-control—are the characteristics of a life that is being transformed by the Holy Spirit. As disciples cultivate their relationship with the Holy Spirit, these qualities begin to flourish in their lives, reflecting the character of Christ. This spiritual fruit is not something that disciples can produce on their own; it is the result of the Holy Spirit's presence and power working within them, shaping their character to resemble that of Jesus.

The development of spiritual fruit through the Holy Spirit is essential for disciples as it not only marks their growth in holiness but also serves as a powerful testimony to others. The fruit of the Spirit impacts every area of life, influencing relationships, decisions, and actions. As disciples grow in love, they become more compassionate and selfless; as they grow in peace, they become more centered and trusting in God's sovereignty. Each aspect of the fruit of the Spirit contributes to a life that glorifies God and fulfills His purpose for His people. Ultimately, the Holy Spirit's role in sanctification is about leading disciples into a deeper, more authentic expression of their faith, enabling them to live out the gospel in everyday life.

Guidance and Wisdom: The Holy Spirit plays a vital role in providing guidance and wisdom to disciples, enabling them to understand God's will and make decisions that align with His righteousness. This divine guidance is not simply about making the right choices in life but about discerning and following the path that God has set out. The Holy Spirit helps disciples navigate the complexities of life by illuminating the truth of God's Word and applying it to their specific circumstances. Through prayer, reflection, and a sensitivity to the Spirit's leading, disciples are equipped to make decisions that honor God and further His kingdom.

One of the key functions of the Holy Spirit is to teach and remind disciples of the teachings of Jesus Christ. In John 14:26, Jesus assures His disciples that the Holy Spirit, whom the Father will send in His name, "shall teach you all things, and bring all things to your remembrance, whatsoever I have said unto you." This promise means that the Holy Spirit continues to guide disciples by bringing to mind the words and teachings of Jesus, ensuring that they stay rooted in the truth. This ongoing instruction is crucial for spiritual growth, as it helps disciples internalize the teachings of Christ and apply them to their lives, even in situations that may not have a clear precedent in Scripture.

Moreover, the Holy Spirit's guidance goes beyond intellectual understanding; it involves a deep, relational knowledge of God's will. As disciples cultivate their relationship with the Holy Spirit, they become more attuned to His voice and more receptive to His leading. This guidance often comes through a sense of conviction, prompting disciples to act in ways that are consistent with God's character and commands. The wisdom imparted by the Holy Spirit is not merely human wisdom but divine insight that empowers disciples to live lives that reflect God's love, holiness, and truth. In this way, the Holy Spirit ensures that disciples remain grounded in their faith, guided by God's wisdom in every aspect of life.

Empowerment for Service: The Holy Spirit plays a crucial role in empowering disciples for service by equipping them with spiritual gifts that enable them to fulfill their roles within the Church and the broader community. These spiritual gifts, which are diverse and uniquely tailored to each individual, are given for the purpose of building up the body of Christ and advancing God's kingdom on earth. The gifts listed in 1 Corinthians 12 and Romans 12 include abilities such as wisdom, knowledge, faith, healing, prophecy, teaching, and leadership. Each gift, though different, is vital to the functioning of the Church, as it allows disciples to serve in ways that complement one another and contribute to the overall mission of spreading the gospel and demonstrating God's love.

The variety of spiritual gifts underscores the Holy Spirit's wisdom in distributing them according to the needs of the Church and the community. Some disciples are given the gift of teaching, enabling them to instruct others in the truths of Scripture, while others might be gifted in administration, helping to organize and manage the Church's activities effectively. Still, others may have the gift of mercy, allowing them to compassionately serve those in need. Regardless of the specific gift, the Holy Spirit empowers each disciple to use their abilities for the common good, fostering unity and growth within the body of Christ. This distribution of gifts ensures that no disciple is left without a role or purpose within the Church, and it highlights the interdependence of the Church's members as they work together to fulfill God's purposes.

Furthermore, the empowerment for service through the Holy Spirit extends beyond the Church to impact the broader community. As disciples exercise their spiritual gifts, they become witnesses of God's grace and power, demonstrating His love in tangible ways. Whether through acts of service, speaking words of encouragement, or leading others in worship, the Holy Spirit enables disciples to be effective ambassadors of Christ in the world. This empowerment not only strengthens the Church internally but also draws others to the faith, as they see the transformative power of God at work in the lives of His people. Ultimately, the Holy Spirit's empowerment for service is a key aspect of fulfilling the Great Commission, as disciples are equipped to go out and make a difference in the world, advancing God's kingdom on earth.

Comfort and Assurance: The Holy Spirit's role as a Comforter is one of His most profound and personal functions in the life of a disciple. He provides a sense of peace that surpasses understanding, even in the midst of trials and uncertainties. This peace comes from the assurance that God's presence is always with us, guiding and protecting us through every circumstance. The Holy Spirit's comforting presence is not just a temporary relief from anxiety but a constant source of strength and calm that anchors our hearts in the love and faithfulness of God.

Romans 8:16 beautifully captures the intimate relationship between the Holy Spirit and disciples by stating that "The Spirit itself beareth witness with our spirit, that we are the children of God." This testimony from the Holy Spirit offers a deep sense of security and belonging, affirming our identity as God's children. This assurance is crucial for disciples as it reinforces their understanding of being loved, valued, and accepted by God. Knowing that we are His children gives us the confidence to approach

God with our needs, fears, and joys, fully trusting in His care and provision.

The comfort and assurance provided by the Holy Spirit also empower disciples to face life's challenges with courage and hope. The awareness of God's unwavering presence allows us to endure difficulties without being overwhelmed by fear or doubt. The Holy Spirit's comforting role serves as a reminder that we are never alone; God is with us, and His Spirit resides within us. This assurance transforms our outlook on life, enabling us to live with a deep sense of peace, purpose, and confidence in God's promises.

Chapter 5: Fruits of the Spirit

The "fruits of the Spirit" are essential characteristics that should naturally emerge in the lives of disciples who are guided by the Holy Spirit. These fruits, described in Galatians 5:22-23, are love, joy, peace, patience, kindness, goodness, faithfulness, gentleness, and self-control. They are not merely virtues to aspire to; they are evidence of the Holy Spirit's active presence and transformative power in the life of a disciple. As disciples grow in their relationship with God, these fruits become more evident, reflecting the character of Christ in their daily actions and interactions.

Love As the first and foremost fruit of the Spirit, is the cornerstone of a disciple's life and character. It is more than a fleeting emotion or affection; it is a deliberate, selfless, and sacrificial commitment to the well-being of others. This love mirrors the love that God has for humanity, a love that is unconditional and all-encompassing. Jesus Himself highlighted love as the greatest commandment, stating that the entire law is fulfilled in loving God with all our heart, soul, and mind, and loving our neighbor as ourselves (Matthew 22:37-40). For disciples, this love is not optional but essential, as it serves as the defining mark of their faith and their relationship with God.

The love that the Holy Spirit produces in disciples is transformative, enabling them to love others unconditionally, even those who may be difficult to love. This kind of love transcends human limitations and is not dependent on the worthiness or actions of the other person. It is a love that seeks the best for others, even at personal cost. This is the love that Jesus demonstrated throughout His life and ministry, ultimately laying down His life for humanity. Through the Holy Spirit, disciples are empowered to embody this same love, showing kindness, compassion, and forgiveness to all, regardless of the circumstances.

Moreover, love as the foundation of the fruits of the Spirit ensures that all other fruits are rooted in a genuine and sincere desire to serve others and honor God. Without love, the other fruits— joy, peace, patience, kindness, goodness, faithfulness, gentleness, and self-control—lack depth and authenticity. Love gives these virtues their true meaning and purpose, as they are all expressions of a heart aligned with God's will. As disciples cultivate this love through the Holy Spirit, they become living testimonies of God's love in the world, reflecting the character of Christ and drawing others to the transformative power of His love.

Joy This fruit emerges from a deep and abiding relationship with God, transcending the fluctuating circumstances of life. Unlike mere happiness, which is often tied to external events and fleeting pleasures, joy is a profound and enduring sense of contentment that is rooted in the assurance of God's presence and His promises. This joy is not contingent upon favorable situations or personal achievements but is a steady and reliable source of inner peace that flows from a secure relationship with God. It is a spiritual joy that remains constant even amidst trials and difficulties, reflecting a heart that is anchored in the certainty of God's unwavering love and faithfulness.

This kind of joy is grounded in the understanding of God's eternal promises and His sovereign control over all aspects of life. When disciples cultivate a relationship with God through prayer, worship, and immersion in His Word, they begin to experience a joy that is not easily shaken by life's challenges. This joy springs from the knowledge that God is always present, guiding and supporting them through every circumstance. It is a joy that recognizes God's ultimate plan for their lives and trusts that He is working all things together for their good, even when the path ahead is uncertain.

Furthermore, joy is a powerful testament to the transformative work of the Holy Spirit in a disciple's life. When disciples exhibit joy in the face of adversity, it serves as a witness to others of the inner strength and hope found in Christ. This joy is not merely a personal experience but a reflection of the divine peace that God imparts to those who walk closely with Him. It encourages others to seek the same relationship with God, illustrating how His presence can profoundly alter one's outlook and bring a deep, lasting happiness that surpasses earthly circumstances.

Peace The fruit of peace, as a manifestation of the Holy Spirit's work in a disciple's life, represents a profound state of inner tranquility that transcends external circumstances. This peace is not merely the absence of conflict or distress but a deep-seated calm that flows from trusting in God's sovereignty and His unwavering care for His people. It is an inner serenity that remains unshaken by the tumultuous events of life, grounded in the assurance that God is in control and working all things together for the good of those who love Him. This peace is a divine gift that assures disciples of God's presence and provision, regardless of the challenges they may face.

For disciples, experiencing peace is essential as they navigate the inevitable trials and tribulations of life. This peace provides the strength needed to remain steadfast in their faith, even when confronted with difficulties that might otherwise lead to anxiety or despair. It allows them to face adversity with a sense of calm and confidence, knowing that their lives are held securely in the hands of a loving and all-powerful God. This tranquility empowers disciples to continue in their mission, to minister effectively, and to live out their faith with integrity and grace, despite the obstacles they may encounter.

Moreover, the peace that the Holy Spirit bestows upon disciples acts as a powerful testimony to others. When disciples demonstrate a calm and composed demeanor in the face of adversity, it reflects the inner peace that comes from a deep trust in God. This peace can attract others to the faith, as it offers a tangible example of how a relationship with God can transform one's response to life's challenges. By embodying this peace, disciples not only strengthen their own spiritual resilience but also become witnesses to the transformative power of God's peace, drawing others to seek the same assurance and tranquility in their own lives.

Long Suffering Also defined as patience, Long Suffering reflects the outward expression of the Holy Spirit's transformative work in a disciple's life. This fruit of the Spirit enables disciples to endure hardships, delays, and challenging situations with a steadfast and gracious attitude. Unlike mere patience, which might be strained by the trials of life, long suffering embodies a profound inner strength and resilience that comes from trusting in God's timing and purposes. It is a manifestation of the Spirit's work that allows disciples to remain calm and composed, even when faced with prolonged difficulties or setbacks, demonstrating a deep-seated faith in God's sovereign plan.

The ability to wait on God's timing without becoming anxious or frustrated is a key aspect of long suffering. This fruit empowers disciples to endure trials with a spirit of hope and perseverance, rather than being overwhelmed by impatience or despair. It reflects a mature and trusting relationship with God, where disciples understand that His timing is perfect, and His plans are for their ultimate good. By cultivating long suffering, disciples exhibit a willingness to embrace God's schedule rather than their own, displaying a trust that God's delays are not denials but opportunities for growth and deeper reliance on Him.

Furthermore, long suffering equips disciples to deal graciously with others, even in difficult situations. This quality is vital for maintaining healthy relationships and fostering a supportive community within the body of Christ. It allows disciples to respond to others with empathy and understanding, rather than reacting with irritation or resentment. By modeling long suffering, disciples reflect the patience and grace of Christ, demonstrating the Spirit's influence in their interactions. This graciousness not only helps to navigate interpersonal challenges but also serves as a witness to the transformative power of the Holy Spirit in their lives, drawing others to the same patience and grace that they themselves have received from God.

Gentleness As a fruit of the Spirit, this quality goes beyond mere good intentions and manifests as a tender and compassionate approach to others. Gentleness involves a readiness to treat others with care and understanding, regardless of their behavior or circumstances. It is an active demonstration of love, seen through thoughtful and considerate interactions. When the Holy Spirit works within a disciple, gentleness becomes a natural overflow of their relationship with God, influencing their actions and interactions in meaningful ways.

The expression of gentleness is not limited to grand gestures but is often found in the everyday moments of life. It involves small acts of grace, such as speaking with kindness, offering a comforting presence, or responding with patience. These acts of gentleness are rooted in a heart transformed by the Holy Spirit, which approaches others with empathy and respect. Such expressions of love in action are indicative of a disciple's commitment to living out the teachings of Christ and embodying His love in their daily lives. Through gentleness, disciples reflect the character of God and make His love visible to those around them.

Moreover, gentleness is a powerful witness to the transformative impact of the Holy Spirit in a disciple's life. It serves as a testament to the inner change that has taken place, revealing the depth of their relationship with God and their alignment with His will. By practicing gentleness, disciples not only build stronger relationships and foster a sense of peace but also draw others to the faith. This outward expression of the Spirit's work demonstrates the practical application of a disciple's love and highlights the impact of the Holy Spirit's influence, making the love of Christ evident in both word and deed.

Goodness This quality is defined by moral integrity and a consistent pursuit of what is right, irrespective of personal gain or recognition. Goodness involves more than just refraining from wrongdoing; it encompasses actively striving to uphold virtue and justice in every aspect of life. When the Holy Spirit is at work in a disciple, their actions and decisions visibly demonstrate a heart devoted to God's principles and a commitment to living according to His standards.

The manifestation of goodness is evident in the disciple's unwavering dedication to honesty, fairness, and compassion. It involves making choices that align with a profound sense of responsibility and a genuine intent to positively impact others. This commitment to righteousness is expressed in daily interactions, from standing firm in truth to providing support for those in need and making ethical decisions. Goodness is therefore more than a transient trait; it is a stable expression of a disciple's character, molded by the Spirit's influence and a desire to fulfill God's will.

Moreover, goodness acts as a compelling testimony to the Holy Spirit's transformative power in a disciple's life. By demonstrating moral integrity and a sincere desire to act rightly, disciples stand out as beacons of virtue in a world often marred by injustice and corruption. Their acts of goodness not only reveal their relationship with God but also serve as a witness to the Spirit's work within them. Through goodness, disciples provide a practical example of how Disciple values can be applied in daily life, showcasing the righteousness and virtue that result from the Holy Spirit's influence.

Faithfulness As a fruit of the Spirit, Faithfulness embodies a deep loyalty and unwavering commitment to God and His word. This virtue is characterized by a steadfast adherence to God's promises and teachings, reflecting a heart that remains devoted even amidst trials and uncertainties. Faithfulness involves consistently aligning one's life with God's principles, demonstrating trust and dedication in all aspects of one's spiritual journey. This loyalty is not only a personal commitment but also a public declaration of a disciple's trust in God's unchanging nature and His faithful promises.

In addition to loyalty to God, faithfulness manifests in reliability within relationships and responsibilities. A faithful disciple is someone who can be counted on to honor their commitments, whether in their personal relationships, professional obligations, or community involvement. This reliability is a testament to the integrity and consistency that define a life influenced by the Holy Spirit. By fulfilling promises, supporting others through challenges, and carrying out responsibilities diligently, disciples showcase the practical outworking of faithfulness in their everyday lives.

Moreover, faithfulness acts as a powerful witness to the transformative effect of the Holy Spirit. It demonstrates the Spirit's influence by producing a life marked by trustworthiness and dedication. This outward expression of faithfulness serves as an example to others, reflecting the steadfast nature of God's own faithfulness. Through consistent loyalty to God and reliable behavior in relationships and duties, disciples exemplify how the Holy Spirit fosters a life of integrity and devotion, thereby drawing others to the same commitment and trust in God.

Meekness As a fruit of the Spirit, Meekness represents a profound quality of humility and gentleness that arises from a deep understanding of one's place before God. Contrary to the common misconception that meekness implies weakness, it actually signifies strength under control. A meek person demonstrates a balanced attitude, where their power and influence are exercised with restraint and grace. This inner quality reflects a heart that is fully aware of its dependence on God, leading to a life marked by gentleness and a willingness to serve others without seeking personal gain or recognition.

The outward expression of meekness is seen in how a disciple interacts with others. It involves responding to criticism, conflict, and personal challenges with calmness and humility, rather than with anger or defensiveness. Meekness is characterized by a patient and non-violent demeanor, even in situations where one's rights or opinions are challenged. This quality allows disciples to build positive relationships and foster a spirit of reconciliation, reflecting Christ's own humility and gentleness. By practicing meekness, disciples embody the teachings of Jesus, who described Himself as "meek and lowly in heart" (Matthew 11:29).

Furthermore, meekness plays a crucial role in the disciple's spiritual growth and witness. It creates an environment where the Holy Spirit can work effectively, allowing the disciple to embody the grace and love of Christ. By embracing meekness, disciples demonstrate a commitment to living out the values of God's kingdom, showing that true strength is found in humility and service. This quality not only enhances personal relationships but also serves as a powerful testimony to others, highlighting the transformative impact of the Holy Spirit in a disciple's life and drawing others towards a life of humility and grace.

Temperance As a fruit of the Spirit, Temperance signifies self-control and moderation, reflecting a disciplined approach to one's desires and actions. This quality involves exercising restraint over impulses and maintaining balance in all aspects of life. Temperance is not merely about abstaining from excess but about cultivating a mindset that values moderation and prudence. It empowers a disciple to make wise decisions and resist temptations, aligning their behavior with God's will and living out the principles of faith with integrity.

The outward expression of temperance is evident in how a disciple manages various aspects of their life, including eating, drinking, and other behaviors that can lead to excess. Temperance involves making choices that reflect self-discipline and a commitment to maintaining harmony and balance. For instance, it is seen in resisting the urge to overindulge in food, drink, or entertainment, and in managing one's time and resources in a way that honors God. By practicing temperance, disciples demonstrate a commitment to living a life that is not driven by unchecked desires but by thoughtful and purposeful decisions.

Moreover, temperance enhances a disciple's spiritual growth and witness. By exhibiting self-control and moderation, disciples show the transformative power of the Holy Spirit at work in their lives. This quality not only fosters personal discipline but also creates a positive example for others to follow. It demonstrates that a life of faith involves not just spiritual zeal but also practical wisdom and self-restraint. Through temperance, disciples reflect the balanced and measured nature of Christ's character, highlighting the impact of the Holy Spirit in shaping a life of harmony and alignment with God's purposes.

Conclusion

The fruits of the Spirit are the visible evidence of the Holy Spirit's work in the life of a disciple. They represent the character of Christ being formed in the disciple, influencing every aspect of their life. As disciples cultivate these fruits, they not only grow in their relationship with God but also become effective witnesses to His love and grace in the world. The fruits of the Spirit are not produced by human effort but by a life surrendered to the Holy Spirit, allowing Him to work through them to reflect the character and love of Christ to those around them.

Chapter 6: Eliminating False Gods

The Holy Spirit plays a crucial role in guiding disciples to discern false gods and remain faithful to the one true God, the God of Abraham, Isaac, and Jacob, and the Father of Jesus Christ. Throughout the Bible, there are numerous warnings against the worship of false gods and idols, emphasizing the importance of staying true to the Most High. The Holy Spirit, as the Spirit of truth, works within the hearts of disciples, helping them to recognize and reject anything that contradicts the teachings of Scripture and the nature of God. In a world where many people are drawn to different gods and images, the Holy Spirit serves as a protector, keeping disciples aligned with the truth and away from the deception of false worship.

One of the primary ways the Holy Spirit helps disciples discern false gods is by guiding them in understanding and applying the truth of Scripture. The Bible clearly teaches that God is spirit and must be worshipped in spirit and in truth (John 4:24). This means that any attempt to represent God through physical images or idols is not only inadequate but also contrary to His nature. The Holy Spirit brings to mind these biblical truths and convicts disciples when they are tempted to engage in practices that involve the worship of false gods or idols. The Spirit enables disciples to see the emptiness and futility of such worship, leading them to a deeper devotion to the true and living God.

In today's world, where people are often exposed to various religious practices and symbols, the Holy Spirit's role in discernment is more critical than ever. Many individuals, sometimes unknowingly, dabble in the worship of gods and idols from different cultures and religions, including those of the Egyptians, Hindus, Catholics, Buddhists, and others. The Holy Spirit provides disciples with the wisdom to see beyond the allure of these practices and to understand that they are not of God. The Spirit helps disciples recognize that true worship involves a personal relationship with God through Jesus Christ and that any other form of worship is ultimately empty and leads away from the truth.

The Bible also provides a key criterion for discerning who is of God: the confession that

Jesus Christ has come in the flesh (1 John 4:2-3). The Holy Spirit enables disciples to test the spirits and recognize whether a teaching or practice aligns with the truth of Jesus Christ. This discernment is essential in a world where many false teachings and idols seek to divert attention away from the true worship of God. The Holy Spirit continually draws disciples back to the centrality of Christ and keeps them grounded in the truth, ensuring that their worship remains pure and focused on the Most High. By relying on the Holy Spirit's guidance, disciples can resist the temptation to worship false gods and remain faithful to the God who revealed Himself through the testament of Jesus Christ.

Pagan Celebrations

The Holy Spirit plays a vital role in leading disciples away from pagan practices that have been integrated into modern Disciple traditions, including celebrations like Easter, Christmas, and Halloween, which have origins rooted in paganism and associations with other gods. Understanding the Holy Spirit's guidance in this area requires a return to the biblical call for purity in worship and a clear distinction between the holy and the profane.

Easter, often celebrated as the resurrection of Jesus, has elements such as eggs and bunnies that trace back to pagan fertility rites and the worship of the goddess Ishtar. Similarly, Christmas, which is said to be for the birth of Christ, is actually from the Roman festival of Saturnalia and the worship of various pagan deities. Halloween, originally known as Samhain, was a Celtic festival marking the end of the harvest season and a time to honor the dead, with connections to various pagan rituals and beliefs in other gods. The Bible strongly warns against blending the worship of the one true God with the practices of other religions. Deuteronomy 12:29-31 emphasizes that God's people are not to inquire about how other nations serve their gods or adopt their practices, as these are considered detestable to the Lord.

The Holy Spirit leads disciples into all truth (John 16:13) and helps them discern the difference between genuine worship and practices that are contrary to God's will. As disciples grow in their relationship with God and their understanding of His Word, the Holy Spirit convicts them to move away from these syncretized traditions and to seek forms of worship that are fully aligned with biblical teachings. This guidance is not merely about rejecting certain holidays but about cultivating a heart that seeks to honor God in spirit and truth (John 4:24), free from the influence of pagan customs. The Holy Spirit empowers disciples to discern these influences, reject them, and choose instead to observe biblical feasts and practices that glorify God alone.

As disciples follow the Holy Spirit's leading, they begin to recognize the importance of maintaining purity in their worship and devotion. This often involves making difficult choices to forsake long-standing cultural traditions that conflict with the teachings of Scripture. By doing so, they align themselves more closely with God's will, avoiding the pitfalls of idolatry and false worship. "Beware lest any man spoil you through philosophy and vain deceit, after the tradition of men, after the rudiments of the world, and not after Christ" Colossians 2:8. The Holy Spirit's work in this area is part of the broader process of sanctification, helping disciples to become more like Christ in every aspect of their lives, including how they celebrate and commemorate significant events.

Chapter 7: Teaching All Truth

The Holy Spirit plays a vital role in leading disciples to all truth, as Jesus promised in John 16:13: "Howbeit when he, the Spirit of truth, is come, he will guide you into all truth." This truth is not abstract but deeply rooted in God's laws, as revealed in the Scriptures. The Bible itself declares, "Thy righteousness is an everlasting righteousness, and thy law is the truth. " (Psalm 119:142), indicating that God's commandments are the foundation of divine truth. Therefore, when the Holy Spirit guides disciples into all truth, He is guiding them to understand, embrace, and keep God's laws.

Apostle Paul refers to the Old Testament law as our "schoolmaster" in Galatians 3:24, highlighting its role in guiding disciples to Christ. Without a solid understanding of the Old Testament laws, disciples may find their understanding of Jesus Christ incomplete or out of context. Jesus Himself emphasized the continuity and importance of the law, stating in Matthew 5:17-19, "Think not that I am come to destroy the law, or the prophets: I am not come to destroy, but to fulfill. For verily I say unto you, Till heaven and earth pass, one jot or one tittle shall in no wise pass from the law, till all be fulfilled. Whosoever therefore shall break one of these least commandments, and shall teach men so, he shall be called the least in the kingdom of heaven." This passage makes it clear that the law remains relevant, and the Holy Spirit guides disciples to understand and keep these commandments as an expression of their love for God.

The 10 Commandments

The Holy Spirit leads disciples to observe the Ten Commandments, which serve as the foundation of moral living and a reflection of God's character. For example, the commandment to "Remember the sabbath day, to keep it holy" (Exodus 20:8) is not just an Old Testament obligation but a timeless principle that the Holy Spirit impresses upon disciples. "Wherefore the children of Israel shall keep the sabbath, to observe the sabbath throughout their generations, *for* a perpetual covenant" Exodus 31:16. Perpetual means forever. The Sabbath is a sign of God's covenant with His people, a day set apart for rest and worship, and a reminder of

God's creative and redemptive work. Similarly, the commandment "Thou shalt not kill" (Exodus 20:13) extends beyond physical murder to include harboring anger or hatred in one's heart, as Jesus taught in Matthew 5:21-22. The Holy Spirit empowers disciples to live out these commandments in their daily lives, not merely as legalistic requirements but as expressions of love for God and neighbor.

The Ten Commandments, given by God to Moses on Mount Sinai, are foundational laws that reflect God's will for His people. They are more than just a set of rules; they are principles that govern the relationship between God and His people, and between individuals within a community. The commandments cover essential aspects of life, such as honoring God alone, keeping the Sabbath, respecting parents, and prohibiting actions like murder, adultery, theft, and bearing false witness. These commandments are timeless and remain relevant, guiding disciples in living a life that honors God and promotes justice and love toward others.

The Holy Spirit plays a crucial role in guiding disciples to follow the Ten Commandments. As the Spirit of truth, the Holy Spirit writes these laws on the hearts of disciples, moving them from mere external observance to an internal commitment to God's moral standards. The Spirit empowers disciples to live in obedience to God's commandments, both out of fear and out of love and a desire to please God. This internal guidance helps disciples understand the deeper implications of the commandments, such as recognizing that anger can lead to the sin of murder in the heart, or that lust is akin to committing adultery.

Moreover, the Holy Spirit provides the strength and conviction needed to uphold these commandments in a world that often opposes them. In situations where disciples face temptations to lie, steal, or engage in idolatry, the Holy Spirit reminds them of the commandments and empowers them to choose righteousness. By guiding disciples in the way of truth and holiness, the Holy Spirit ensures that the commandments are not just rules to be followed but are embraced as a way of life that reflects the character of God. In this way, the Ten Commandments remain a vital part of the disciple's walk with God, sustained and fulfilled through the Holy Spirit's work in their lives.

Social Laws

God's social laws, as outlined in the Bible, establish the principles of justice, fairness, and compassion that should govern relationships within society. These laws address how people should treat one another, particularly in matters of justice, charity, and social responsibility. For instance, the laws concerning the treatment of the poor, the protection of widows and orphans, and the fair treatment of workers are central to God's vision for a just society. The Holy Spirit plays a crucial role in guiding disciples to uphold these social laws, leading them to act justly, love mercy, and walk humbly with God in their interactions with others.

The Holy Spirit not only convicts disciples of the importance of these social laws but also empowers them to live them out in practical ways. For example, the biblical principle of loving one's neighbor as oneself is not just a personal ethic but a call to social action. The Holy Spirit moves disciples to advocate for justice, care for the marginalized, and work towards a society that reflects God's righteousness. This might involve supporting the needy, standing against exploitation, or promoting peace and reconciliation in conflict situations. Through the guidance of the Holy Spirit, disciples are equipped to fulfill their social responsibilities in a way that honors God and benefits others.

Moreover, the Holy Spirit fosters a sense of community among disciples, encouraging them to support and hold one another accountable to God's social laws. This communal aspect of discipleship ensures that social justice is not just an individual pursuit but a collective effort within the body of Christ. The early Church, for example, demonstrated this by sharing their resources to ensure that no one was in need. This spirit-led approach to social responsibility continues today as disciples, guided by the Holy Spirit, seek to create communities and societies that embody the justice, compassion, and fairness that God desires. Through their commitment to God's social laws, disciples become living witnesses to the transformative power of the Holy Spirit in building a just and loving society.

Moral Laws

Moral laws, as outlined in the Bible, form the ethical foundation for how disciples should live in relation to God and others. These laws, which include principles such as honesty, justice, mercy, and sexual purity, reflect God's character and His desire for His people to live in a way that is pleasing to Him. The Holy Spirit plays a vital role in leading disciples to follow these moral laws by convicting them of sin, guiding them in righteousness, and empowering them to live lives that honor God. Through the Holy Spirit, disciples are not only aware of what is right and wrong but are also given the strength and desire to choose what is right.

The Holy Spirit's guidance in following moral laws goes beyond mere external obedience; it involves a transformation of the heart. For example, while the moral law prohibits lying, the Holy Spirit works within disciples to cultivate a love for truth and integrity, making honesty a natural expression of their character. Similarly, the commandment to love one's neighbor as oneself is not just a rule to be followed but becomes a genuine concern for others' well-being, motivated by the Holy Spirit's presence in their lives. This internal transformation leads to a deeper understanding and practice of moral laws, aligning disciples' lives more closely with God's will.

In addition to guiding individual behavior, the Holy Spirit also leads disciples to uphold and advocate for moral principles in the broader community. This involves standing against injustice, defending the oppressed, and promoting peace and reconciliation. By following the Holy Spirit's leading, disciples become agents of God's righteousness in the world, reflecting His moral laws in their actions and influencing others to do the same. The moral laws, therefore, are not just personal guidelines but are part of the disciple's calling to be salt and light in a world that often disregards God's standards.

Dietary Laws

In addition to the moral law, the Holy Spirit also guides disciples to observe the dietary laws. The dietary laws outlined in the Old Testament, particularly in Leviticus 11 and Deuteronomy 14, were given by God to the Israelites as part of His covenant with them. These laws distinguish between clean and unclean animals, providing guidelines on what could be consumed and what should be avoided. For example, animals that chew the cud and have split hooves, such as cattle and sheep, are considered clean, while others like pigs and camels are deemed unclean. Similarly, certain birds, fish with fins and scales, and specific insects are allowed, while others such as shrimp and lobster are prohibited. These dietary laws served not only as health guidelines but also as a way to set the Israelites apart as a holy people, dedicated to God in every aspect of their lives, including their eating habits. Today's disciples, which include gentiles that are grafted in, are called to remain set apart with clean living.

The significance of these dietary laws extends beyond mere physical health; they symbolize the call to holiness and separation from sin. By adhering to these dietary restrictions, disciples are reminded daily of their unique identity as God's people, distinct from the surrounding nations. The act of choosing what to eat is part of the obedience, reflecting a commitment to live according to God's commands. This separation also points to the spiritual truth that God's people are to be set apart in all areas of life, avoiding what is spiritually unclean and embracing what is pure and righteous.

In the New Testament, the discussion around dietary laws shifts, particularly with the teachings of Jesus and the apostles. While Jesus declared that what defiles a person comes from the heart rather than from what they eat (Mark 7:15), the principle of holiness remains central. The dietary laws continue to hold importance. They remind disciples of the need to discern between what is spiritually clean and unclean, to live lives that honor God in all things, and to be mindful of how their choices reflect their commitment to holiness. The Holy Spirit guides disciples in understanding the deeper spiritual significance of these laws, leading them to live in a way that is pleasing to God.

The Passover Lamb

Jesus is often referred to as the Passover Lamb, a title that highlights His role in fulfilling the sacrificial system established in the Old Testament. Just as the Passover lamb was sacrificed to save the Israelites from death during their exodus from Egypt, Jesus was sacrificed to deliver humanity from the bondage of sin and death. The Apostle Paul explicitly connects Jesus to this imagery, stating in 1 Corinthians 5:7, "For even Christ our Passover is sacrificed for us." Furthermore, Jesus is also seen as the "first fruits" of those who have risen from the dead (1 Corinthians 15:20). In ancient Israel, the Feast of First Fruits was a celebration of the first harvest, symbolizing the beginning of a greater harvest to come. In the same way, Jesus' resurrection is the first instance of eternal life, promising a future resurrection for all who belong to Him.

The Holy Spirit plays a crucial role in leading disciples to the truth of these significant Biblical feasts and their fulfillment in Christ. The Holy Spirit guides disciples to understand and appreciate the deep connections between Jesus and the Passover, First Fruits, Unleavened Bread, Pentecost, and other days of remembrance. These observances, originally given to Israel as a means of commemorating God's acts of salvation, take on even greater significance when viewed through the lens of Christ's life, death, and resurrection. Through the Holy Spirit, disciples gain a deeper understanding of these holy days, recognizing them not just as historical events but as ongoing spiritual realities that point to the work of Jesus and the fulfillment of God's redemptive plan.

The Love of God

Many people today claim to love God but neglect His commandments, which goes against the teachings of Scripture. As 1 John 5:3 states, "For this is the love of God, that we keep his commandments: and his commandments are not grievous." The Holy Spirit, as the Spirit of truth, leads disciples to a love that is demonstrated through obedience to God's laws. This obedience is not burdensome but a joy and privilege, as it reflects a heart transformed by the Holy Spirit and aligned with God's will. In this way, the Holy Spirit continually guides disciples into all truth, leading them to live in accordance with God's laws and to experience the fullness of life in Christ.

Chapter 8: Conviction of Sin

The Holy Spirit plays a critical role in convicting individuals of sin, guiding them toward righteousness, and discerning judgment. According to John 16:8, "And when he is come, he will reprove the world of sin, and of righteousness, and of judgment." This conviction is a profound, internal awareness that helps disciples recognize their moral failings and aligns their lives with God's standards. The Holy Spirit's work in this area is essential for spiritual growth and transformation, as it leads individuals to confront and amend their sinful behaviors while drawing closer to God.

The process of conviction by the Holy Spirit often involves an inner prompting or unease that goes beyond mere human conscience. For example, when a disciple is faced with a moral dilemma, such as whether to engage in premarital sex, the Holy Spirit may bring a sense of conviction that such actions are inconsistent with God's commands. Despite societal norms or personal justifications that a boyfriend or girlfriend might offer, the Holy Spirit's guidance will align with biblical teachings, reinforcing the sanctity of marriage and chastity before it. This internal nudge is not merely a matter of guilt but a call to adhere to divine principles and live in a manner that honors God.

The Holy Spirit also convicts disciples in more subtle ways, such as when dealing with issues of honesty, integrity, and justice. For instance, if a disciple is tempted to cheat on a tax return or engage in deceptive business practices, the Holy Spirit may bring a profound sense of discomfort and remind them of the importance of honesty as outlined in Scripture. This conviction is crucial in prompting disciples to act righteously, even when it might not be convenient or easy. Through this divine guidance, the Holy Spirit helps disciples navigate complex situations, offering wisdom that is grounded in God's Word and leading them towards decisions that reflect His will.

In all these instances, the role of the Holy Spirit as a convictor of sin is to guide disciples toward a path of righteousness and to keep their conscience aligned with God's moral framework. This process of conviction fosters a deeper relationship with God, as it encourages ongoing repentance and transformation. It is a vital aspect of spiritual maturity, helping individuals to continually refine their character and actions in accordance with divine truth. By yielding to the Holy Spirit's conviction, disciples are empowered to live lives that are pleasing to God and reflective of His holiness.

The Bible provides several vivid examples of the Holy Spirit's conviction in the lives of individuals, illustrating how this divine guidance leads to repentance and transformation. One prominent example is found in the story of King David, particularly following his adultery with Bathsheba and the arranged death of her husband, Uriah. The prophet Nathan, under the inspiration of the Holy Spirit, confronts David with a parable that reveals the gravity of his sins (2 Samuel 12:1-14). David's immediate response is one of deep remorse and repentance, acknowledging his sin against God. This episode highlights how the Holy Spirit uses prophetic voices to bring conviction and prompt genuine repentance, steering individuals back to righteousness.

Another significant example of the Holy Spirit's convicting work is seen in the New Testament during the Day of Pentecost. After Peter's powerful sermon, delivered under the anointing of the Holy Spirit, the crowd is "pricked in their heart" and asks, "What shall we do?" (Acts 2:37). This profound conviction leads them to repentance and baptism, marking the birth of the early Church. The Holy Spirit's role here is pivotal, as His presence not only empowers Peter's message but also brings an undeniable sense of urgency and guilt over sin, resulting in the transformation of thousands of lives.

The Apostle Paul's encounter on the road to Damascus serves as another example of the Holy Spirit's conviction. Saul, who later becomes Paul, is struck by a blinding light and hears the voice of Jesus asking, "Saul, Saul, why persecutest thou me?" (Acts 9:4-6). This dramatic encounter leads to Saul's conversion and subsequent calling as a servant of Christ. The Holy Spirit's intervention in this moment not only convicts Saul of his sins but also redirects his life toward a new mission. This transformation underscores the Holy Spirit's powerful role in guiding individuals from a path of error to one of divine purpose and service.

Chapter 9: Spiritual Warfare

In an era where the world exerts a powerful influence over the morals and social norms of many, the need for spiritual discernment and resilience has never been more critical. As disciples navigate these challenging times, the Holy Spirit plays a crucial role in spiritual warfare, equipping and empowering them to stand firm against the forces of darkness. The Apostle Paul's exhortation to "put on the whole armor of God" (Ephesians 6:11) serves as a timeless reminder that disciples are engaged in a spiritual battle, one that requires divine protection and strength. The Holy Spirit, as an active and dynamic presence in the life of a Disciple, is essential in this battle, guiding, empowering, and enabling disciples to resist the enemy's attacks and remain unspotted from the world.

The Armor of God and the Holy Spirit

Paul's depiction of the "whole armor of God" in Ephesians 6:10-18 is a vivid metaphor for the spiritual resources that God provides to disciple s. Each piece of armor symbolizes a different aspect of spiritual readiness and protection. The belt of truth, the breastplate of righteousness, the shoes of the gospel of peace, the shield of faith, the helmet of salvation, and the sword of the Spirit are all vital components of this divine armor. However, it is the Holy Spirit who brings these pieces to life, empowering disciples to use them effectively in spiritual warfare.

The Belt of Truth

The belt of truth, as described by the Apostle Paul in Ephesians 6:14, is the first piece of the armor of God that disciples are instructed to put on in their spiritual warfare. This metaphorical belt represents the foundational role that truth plays in the life of a Disciple. Just as a physical belt holds together and secures a soldier's armor, the truth of God holds together and fortifies the disciple 's spiritual armor, providing stability and coherence to their entire walk of faith. The truth is not merely an abstract concept but is embodied in the person of Jesus Christ, who declared, "I am the way, the truth, and the life" (John 14:6). To put on the belt of truth is to live in the reality of God's Word, allowing it to shape one's thoughts, actions, and identity.

Wearing the belt of truth also means embracing a life of integrity and sincerity. In a world often characterized by deception, falsehood, and moral relativism, the belt of truth distinguishes the disciple as someone committed to honesty and authenticity. This commitment to truth begins with a personal acceptance of God's truth as revealed in Scripture and extends to how disciples conduct themselves in their relationships and interactions. The Holy Spirit, who is the Spirit of truth, aids disciples in discerning truth from falsehood, ensuring that they are not swayed by the lies and temptations of the enemy. When the belt of truth is securely fastened, it protects the disciple from being led astray by the deceitful schemes of the devil, enabling them to stand firm in their faith.

Moreover, the belt of truth empowers disciples to confront the lies of the enemy with confidence and clarity. Satan, described in Scripture as the "father of lies" (John 8:44), often attacks disciple s by distorting the truth and sowing seeds of doubt and confusion. However, when the belt of truth is firmly in place, disciples are equipped to counter these lies with the truth of God's Word. This truth exposes and dismantles the enemy's deceptions, allowing disciples to remain grounded in their faith and focused on their spiritual mission. In this way, the belt of truth not only secures the disciple 's spiritual armor but also serves as a powerful weapon in the ongoing battle against the forces of darkness.

The Breastplate of Righteousness

The breastplate of righteousness, as described in Ephesians 6:14, is a vital component of the armor of God that protects the disciple's heart and vital spiritual organs from the attacks of the enemy. Just as a physical breastplate shields a soldier from fatal blows in battle, the breastplate of righteousness guards the disciple 's inner life—emotions, will, and soul—against the assaults of sin and guilt. This righteousness is not something that disciple s can produce on their own; it is the righteousness of Christ that is imputed to them through faith. When disciples accept Christ as King, His righteousness covers them, allowing them to stand before God not in their own merit, but in the perfect righteousness of Christ.

Wearing the breastplate of righteousness also involves living a life that reflects the righteousness of Christ. It means aligning one's actions, decisions, and character with the standards of holiness and justice that God has set forth. The Holy Spirit plays a crucial role in this process by sanctifying the disciple, gradually transforming them to become more like Christ. As disciples pursue a righteous life, they become more resilient to the temptations and accusations of the enemy, who often seeks to undermine their confidence and lead them into sin. By choosing to live righteously, disciples reinforce their spiritual defenses, making it harder for the enemy's attacks to penetrate their hearts.

Moreover, the breastplate of righteousness offers protection against the condemnation that Satan tries to bring into the lives of disciple s. The enemy often attempts to remind disciples of their past sins and failures, seeking to burden them with guilt and shame. However, the breastplate of righteousness assures disciple s that they are justified before God through Christ's sacrifice. Romans 8:1 affirms, "There is therefore now no condemnation for those who are in Christ Jesus." This assurance gives disciples the confidence to stand firm in their identity as children of God, knowing that their righteousness is secure in Christ. With this confidence, they can resist the enemy's attempts to sow doubt and discouragement, standing firm in the truth that they are clothed in the righteousness of Christ.

The Shoes of the Gospel of Peace

The "shoes of the gospel of peace," mentioned in Ephesians 6:15, represent the readiness and stability that comes from embracing and proclaiming the gospel. Just as shoes provide a soldier with a firm footing and the ability to move confidently in battle, the gospel of peace equips disciple s to stand securely in their faith and to walk boldly in their spiritual journey. The gospel is the good news of Jesus Christ—His life and teachings as well as his death and resurrection—which brings reconciliation between humanity and God. This message of peace is not just a comforting thought but a powerful truth that transforms lives and gives disciples the assurance and strength to face the challenges of life with confidence.

Wearing the shoes of the gospel of peace also symbolizes the disciple 's readiness to share this message with others. The gospel is not meant to be kept to oneself but to be proclaimed to the world. The shoes signify the willingness and eagerness to take the message of peace wherever it is needed. In a world filled with conflict, division, and unrest, the gospel offers true peace—a peace that surpasses all understanding and is rooted in a restored relationship with God. As disciple s carry this message to others, they become agents of God's peace, bringing hope and healing to those who are lost, broken, or searching for meaning.

Furthermore, the shoes of the gospel of peace provide disciples with stability in the midst of spiritual warfare. The enemy often tries to shake the foundation of a disciple 's faith, sowing doubt, fear, and confusion. However, the gospel of peace provides a solid foundation that keeps disciple s grounded in the truth of who God is and what He has done through Christ. This peace is not dependent on external circumstances but on the unchanging nature of God's love and the assurance of His salvation. As disciples stand firm in this peace, they are able to resist the enemy's attempts to destabilize them, maintaining their spiritual balance and moving forward in their mission with purpose and resolve.

The Shield of Faith

The shield of faith, as described in Ephesians 6:16, is a crucial element of the armor of God, providing protection against the relentless attacks of the enemy. In ancient warfare, a shield was the first line of defense, designed to intercept and deflect incoming arrows, spears, and other projectiles. Similarly, the shield of faith serves as the disciple 's primary defense against the "fiery darts" of the evil one—temptations, doubts, fears, and accusations. Faith, in this context, is the confident trust in God's promises, character, and power. When disciple s hold up the shield of faith, they are able to block and extinguish the fiery arrows that Satan hurls their way, preventing them from taking root in their hearts and minds.

The shield of faith is not just a passive defense but an active, dynamic tool that requires the disciple 's constant engagement. Faith is not stagnant; it grows and strengthens as disciple s deepen their relationship with God and immerse themselves in His Word. The more they trust in God's faithfulness, the more effective their shield becomes in deflecting the enemy's attacks. When doubts arise, it is through faith that disciple s remind themselves of God's unchanging nature and His promises to be with them, to protect them, and to bring them through every trial. This active trust in God transforms the shield of faith into a powerful means of resisting the enemy, allowing disciple s to stand firm even in the face of overwhelming opposition.

Moreover, the shield of faith offers communal protection, as it is strengthened in the fellowship of other disciples. In Roman warfare, soldiers would often link their shields together to form a wall of defense, providing greater protection for the entire group. Similarly, the faith of individual disciples is bolstered when they stand together in unity, supporting and encouraging one another. Corporate worship, prayer, and fellowship strengthen the collective faith of the Church, making it more resilient to the enemy's attacks. As disciples gather together, sharing their testimonies and praying for one another, they help to reinforce each other's shields, creating a strong, united front against the forces of darkness. In this way, the shield of faith not only protects the individual disciple but also contributes to the strength and security of the entire community of disciples.

The Helmet of Salvation

The helmet of salvation, described in Ephesians 6:17, is a vital piece of the armor of God that protects the mind of the disciple from spiritual attacks. Just as a physical helmet shields a soldier's head—the most critical and vulnerable part of the body—the helmet of salvation guards the disciple 's thoughts, ensuring that they are secure in their identity in Christ. Salvation, in this context, refers not only to the initial experience of being saved but also to the ongoing assurance of that salvation. The knowledge that in keeping the commandments one is eternally secure in Christ is a powerful defense against the doubts, fears, and lies that the enemy seeks to plant in the mind. By wearing the helmet of salvation, disciples can stand firm, knowing that their ultimate destiny is in God's hands, regardless of the circumstances they face.

The helmet of salvation also emphasizes the importance of protecting the mind from the influence of the world and the enemy's deceit. The battlefield of spiritual warfare often centers on the mind, where thoughts, beliefs, and attitudes are formed. The enemy frequently targets the mind with lies and distortions, attempting to undermine the disciple's faith and lead them into confusion and despair. However, the helmet of salvation, secured by the truth of God's Word and the assurance of eternal life, acts as a safeguard against these attacks. It helps disciple s to filter their thoughts through the lens of God's truth, rejecting anything that does not align with the reality of their salvation and identity in Christ. This mental protection is crucial for maintaining spiritual clarity and focus in the midst of the world's distractions and deceptions.

Furthermore, the helmet of salvation empowers disciples to live with confidence and hope, even in the face of trials and persecution. The assurance of salvation is a source of immense strength, enabling disciple s to endure hardships with the knowledge that their suffering is temporary and that their future is secure in Christ. This hope of salvation sustains disciple s through the darkest of times, giving them the courage to persevere and remain faithful to God's calling. The helmet of salvation, therefore, is not only a defensive tool but also a symbol of the hope and confidence that disciples have in Christ. It reminds them that their salvation is in their hands, through their own faith and works and that nothing can separate them from the love of God (Romans 8:38-39). With this assurance firmly in place, disciple s can face any challenge with a calm and steadfast mind, knowing that their ultimate victory is already won in Christ.

The Sword of the Spirit

The sword of the Spirit, as described in Ephesians 6:17, is a unique piece of the armor of God because it is both an offensive and defensive weapon. Unlike the other pieces of armor, which are primarily for protection, the sword is meant for actively engaging the enemy. The sword of the Spirit is explicitly identified as the Word of God, making it a powerful tool for disciple s to wield in spiritual warfare. The Word of God, inspired by the Holy Spirit, is living and active, sharper than any double-edged sword (Hebrews 4:12). It has the power to cut through deception, convict of sin, and reveal the truth. When disciple s speak or meditate on Scripture, they are wielding the sword of the Spirit, effectively countering the lies and attacks of the enemy with God's truth.

The sword of the Spirit is essential for defending against the specific attacks of the enemy. When Jesus was tempted by Satan in the wilderness, He responded to each temptation with Scripture, saying, "It is written..." (Matthew 4:1-11). This example shows how the Word of God can be used to refute the enemy's lies and resist temptation. By knowing and declaring Scripture, disciples can expose the enemy's tactics and stand firm in their faith. The sword of the Spirit is not just about memorizing verses but about understanding and applying the truth of God's Word in every situation. It allows disciple s to fight back against spiritual attacks with precision and authority, cutting down anything that opposes God's will.

Moreover, the sword of the Spirit is a weapon for advancing the kingdom of God. As disciple s share the gospel and speak God's Word into the lives of others, they are wielding the sword of the Spirit to break down strongholds, bring conviction, and lead people to Christ. The Word of God has the power to transform hearts and minds, bringing light into darkness and freedom to those who are bound by sin. In this way, the sword of the Spirit is not only for personal defense but also for taking ground in the spiritual battle, pushing back the forces of evil, and expanding God's influence in the world. Through the effective use of the sword of the Spirit, disciples participate in God's redemptive work, cutting through the spiritual opposition to bring about His purposes on earth.

Standing Firm in a World of Moral Compromise

In these days and times, when the world exerts such a strong grip on the moral and social norms of society, it is easy for disciples to become entangled in the ways of the world. The influence of secular culture can lead to moral compromise, diluting the distinctiveness of a disciples walk if his or her guard is down. The Armor of God is the disciple's ally in this battle, providing the discernment and strength needed to resist conformity to the world. Paul admonishes disciples in Romans 12:2, "Do not be conformed to this world, but be transformed by the renewal of your mind." This transformation is the work of the Holy Spirit, who renews the disciple 's mind and enables them to discern and embrace God's will, even in the face of cultural pressures.

The Holy Spirit also empowers disciple s to stand firm in their convictions, even when those convictions are at odds with societal norms. This stand is not merely a matter of willpower but is the result of the Spirit's work in fortifying the disciple 's faith and resolve. The Spirit emboldens disciple s to speak the truth in love, to resist the temptation to compromise their values, and to live in a manner that reflects the holiness and righteousness of God. Through the Holy Spirit, disciples are equipped to be salt and light in the world, maintaining their distinctiveness and integrity in the midst of moral decay.

The Role of Prayer in Spiritual Warfare

Prayer is a powerful weapon in spiritual warfare, and it is through the Holy Spirit that disciples are empowered to pray effectively. Paul concludes his discussion of the armor of God with a call to "pray in the Spirit on all occasions with all kinds of prayers and requests" (Ephesians 6:18). This exhortation underscores the importance of prayer in the life of a disciple, especially in the context of spiritual warfare. Praying in the Spirit means praying under the guidance and influence of the Holy Spirit, who intercedes for disciples according to the will of God (Romans 8:26-27).

The Holy Spirit helps disciples to pray with clarity, focus, and power, aligning their prayers with God's purposes and enabling them to stand firm against the enemy's schemes. The Spirit also strengthens the disciple 's perseverance in prayer, ensuring that they do not grow weary in their spiritual battle. Through prayer, the disciple remains connected to God, drawing on His strength and protection in the face of spiritual opposition. In this way, prayer becomes both a defensive and offensive weapon, shielding the disciple from the enemy's attacks while also advancing God's kingdom on earth.

Conclusion

The Holy Spirit plays a vital role in spiritual warfare, empowering disciples to stand firm against the forces of darkness and remain unspotted from the world. The armor of God is made effective through the Holy Spirit's presence and work in the disciple's life. The Holy Spirit not only equips disciples with the spiritual resources they need but also guides, empowers, and sustains them in their battle against the enemy. As disciples navigate a world that increasingly opposes God's truth and values, the Holy Spirit is their constant companion, ensuring that they remain steadfast, courageous, and victorious in their spiritual warfare. Through the Holy Spirit, disciples are enabled to live out their faith boldly, standing as a testament to God's power and grace in a world that desperately needs His light.

Chapter 10: The Gifts of the Holy Spirit

The gifts of the Holy Spirit are special abilities given by God to disciple s for the edification of the church and the fulfillment of His divine purposes on earth. These gifts are distributed by the Holy Spirit according to His will, and each disciple is given at least one gift to serve the body of Christ. The Apostle Paul provides a comprehensive list of these gifts in several of his epistles, most notably in 1 Corinthians 12, Romans 12, and Ephesians 4. The purpose of these gifts is to equip the saints for the work of ministry, to build up the body of Christ, and to foster unity and maturity among disciple s.

The Biblical Basis for Spiritual Gifts

The concept of spiritual gifts is rooted in the New Testament, where the Apostle Paul outlines the various gifts and their functions. In 1 Corinthians 12:4-7, Paul writes, "There are different kinds of gifts, but the same Spirit distributes them. There are different kinds of service, but the same Lord. There are different kinds of working, but in all of them and in everyone it is the same God at work.

Now to each one the manifestation of the Spirit is given for the common good." This passage emphasizes that all gifts, though diverse in nature, originate from the same Holy Spirit and are intended for the common good of the church.

The specific gifts mentioned in the New Testament include, but are not limited to:

The Word of Wisdom: The gift of the word of wisdom is a spiritual gift that allows disciples to speak with divine insight and understanding in situations that require discernment and guidance. Unlike general human wisdom, which comes from experience and knowledge, the word of wisdom is a supernatural gift given by the Holy Spirit to reveal God's will and purpose in a specific moment. This gift often manifests when a person faces a complex problem or decision, and God imparts the wisdom needed to navigate the situation effectively. For example, in Acts 6, the apostles displayed the word of wisdom by appointing deacons to manage the church's daily affairs, allowing them to focus on prayer and ministry of the Word. This decision was not just practical but inspired by divine wisdom, ensuring the church's growth and unity.

The word of wisdom is particularly valuable in leadership, counseling, and situations where strategic decisions must be made. It can provide clarity in times of confusion and offer solutions that align with God's broader plans. This gift can also be a source of encouragement, as it reassures disciple s that God is actively involved in their lives, guiding them through challenging circumstances. However, it is essential for those who receive and share words of wisdom to do so with humility and love, recognizing that this gift is meant to serve others and glorify God, rather than elevate the individual. When exercised correctly, the word of wisdom can be a powerful tool for building up the body of Christ and advancing His kingdom.

The Word of Knowledge: The gift of the word of knowledge is a spiritual gift that enables disciples to receive and share specific, divinely-revealed information that they could not have known through natural means. This gift allows disciples to understand hidden truths or facts that are pertinent to a particular situation or person, often leading to deeper insight, conviction, or encouragement. For instance, in John 4, Jesus displayed the word of knowledge when He told the Samaritan woman at the well about her personal life, revealing that He knew she had five husbands and was living with a man who was not her husband. This knowledge, given by the Holy Spirit, opened the door for a profound conversation that led to her recognition of Jesus as the Messiah and ultimately to the transformation of her life.

For disciples, the word of knowledge is a powerful tool for ministry, particularly in evangelism, counseling, and intercession. When used with discernment and sensitivity, it can bring clarity and conviction, guiding others to a deeper understanding of God's will and drawing them closer to Christ. However, it is important for disciples to exercise this gift with humility and a heart aligned with God's purposes. The goal is always to edify others, strengthen faith, and advance the gospel, not to showcase the gift itself. When disciples faithfully steward the word of knowledge, it can lead to transformative encounters, confirming God's presence and involvement in the lives of individuals and communities.

Faith: The gift of faith is a special manifestation of the Holy Spirit that equips disciples with an extraordinary level of trust and confidence in God's promises and purposes. This gift enables disciple s to believe in the impossible, to stand firm in the face of overwhelming odds, and to inspire others to trust in God's power and provision. Unlike general faith, which is foundational to the disciple's life, the gift of faith is often activated in specific situations where God's will needs to be declared or acted upon with boldness. For example, when Peter walked on water at Jesus' command (Matthew 14:28-29), he exhibited the gift of faith, stepping out in confidence despite the natural impossibility of the situation. This kind of faith is contagious and can encourage others to step out in faith, trusting God for great things.

For disciples, the gift of faith is particularly valuable in ministry and leadership, as it empowers them to move forward with divine confidence, even when circumstances seem insurmountable. This gift enables disciples to trust God's guidance, provision, and timing, leading them to make bold decisions that align with His will. Moreover, the gift of faith often accompanies other spiritual gifts, such as healing or miracles, as it provides the unwavering belief needed to see God's power manifest in extraordinary ways. However, it is important for disciples to exercise this gift with humility, always aligning their faith with God's Word and His character, and recognizing that the outcome rests in His sovereign hands. When used faithfully, the gift of faith can lead to significant breakthroughs in the life of the church and in the advancement of God's kingdom.

Healing: The gift of healing is a spiritual gift bestowed by the Holy Spirit that enables disciples to be instruments of God's miraculous power in restoring physical, emotional, or spiritual health. This gift reflects God's compassion and desire for wholeness, allowing disciple s to pray for and minister to those who are suffering from various ailments. The New Testament is filled with examples of this gift in action, such as when Peter and John healed the lame man at the temple gate in Acts 3, leading to his physical restoration and a powerful testimony of God's power. The gift of healing serves as a tangible expression of God's love and a sign that His kingdom is breaking into the world, bringing life and restoration where there was once brokenness.

For disciples, the gift of healing is a profound tool for ministry, not only bringing relief to those who are in pain but also pointing them to the ultimate healer, Jesus Christ. When exercised with faith, compassion, and humility, this gift can lead to dramatic transformations in the lives of individuals, drawing many to faith in Christ. However, it is important for disciples to recognize that the gift of healing operates according to God's will and timing. While the gift can lead to miraculous recoveries, it is not guaranteed that every prayer for healing will result in immediate or visible results. Sometime God may even decide to end a life and bring a person home. Disciples must trust in God's sovereign plan, understanding that sometimes healing may come in unexpected ways or in the fullness of time. The gift of healing, when used wisely, becomes a powerful witness to God's ongoing work in the world and a means of demonstrating His love and care for His people.

Miracles: The gift of miracles is a powerful spiritual gift through which the Holy Spirit enables disciples to perform extraordinary acts that defy natural laws, demonstrating God's supernatural power and authority. This gift is often manifested in situations where God's intervention is needed to reveal His glory, confirm His message, or provide deliverance. Biblical examples of the gift of miracles include Jesus turning water into wine (John 2:1-11), the multiplication of loaves and fishes to feed thousands (Matthew 14:15-21), and the apostle Paul raising Eutychus from the dead after he fell from a window (Acts 20:9-12). These miraculous events serve as tangible signs of God's presence and power, drawing people to faith and reinforcing the truth of the gospel.

For disciples, the gift of miracles is a profound tool for ministry that can bring about divine interventions in critical situations. This gift often works in conjunction with other spiritual gifts, such as faith or healing, to accomplish God's purposes in the world. Disciples who are entrusted with the gift of miracles are called to steward it with humility and discernment, always seeking to glorify God rather than draw attention to themselves. The gift of miracles can be a catalyst for evangelism, as it often leads to awe and wonder, opening hearts to the reality of God's kingdom. However, it is essential for disciples to recognize that miracles are ultimately at God's discretion, and their primary purpose is to point people to Him, rather than to simply amaze or entertain.

Prophecy: The gift of prophecy is a spiritual gift that allows disciples to receive and communicate messages from God, often providing guidance, encouragement, correction, or insight into future events. Prophecy is a powerful tool in the life of the church, as it helps disciples discern God's will and navigate the complexities of life with divine insight. For disciples, the gift of prophecy is not just about predicting the future but about speaking forth God's truth in a way that aligns with His Word and His character. True prophecy will always align with God's laws and commandments, reflecting His holiness, justice, and love. Any message that contradicts Scripture or leads people away from God's commandments is considered false prophecy and must be rejected.

For those who possess the gift of prophecy, it is crucial to exercise it with humility, discernment, and a deep reverence for God's Word. Prophets in the early church, like Agabus in Acts 11:27-28, provided vital direction and warnings to the disciples, which were consistent with God's revealed will. Similarly, modern disciples with the gift of prophecy must ensure that their messages are rooted in Scripture and tested against the truth of God's commandments. This gift should be used to edify the church, build up the faith of disciples, and draw people closer to God. It's also important for disciples to be open to the guidance of the Holy Spirit and to seek confirmation from the broader church community when sharing prophetic messages, ensuring that they remain faithful to God's purposes and avoid leading others astray.

Discerning of Spirits: The gift of discerning of spirits is a crucial spiritual gift that enables disciples to distinguish between the various spiritual influences at work, whether they are from the Holy Spirit, demonic forces, or human origin. This gift is particularly important in a world where spiritual deception is prevalent, allowing disciples to identify false teachings, deceptive practices, and the presence of evil spirits. Disciples with this gift are equipped to see beyond the surface of situations and discern the true spiritual nature behind actions, words, or events. For example, in Acts 16:16-18, Paul demonstrated the gift of discerning of spirits when he recognized that the spirit speaking through a slave girl was demonic, even though she appeared to be proclaiming truth. His discernment led to the girl's deliverance and a clear witness to the power of God.

For disciples, the gift of discerning of spirits is vital for maintaining the purity and truth of the church. It allows them to protect themselves and others from spiritual deception, ensuring that their teachings and practices align with God's Word. This gift also aids in spiritual warfare, helping disciples recognize and counteract the strategies of the enemy. Disciples must use this gift with wisdom and humility, relying on the Holy Spirit's guidance to correctly interpret what they discern and respond appropriately. It is also important for those with this gift to work in unity with the broader church community, testing their discernment against Scripture and seeking counsel from trusted leaders. When exercised faithfully, the gift of discerning of spirits can safeguard the church and empower disciples to walk in truth and spiritual freedom.

Speaking in Tongues: The gift of speaking in tongues, as described in the Bible, is the supernatural ability given by the Holy Spirit to speak in actual human languages that the speaker has never learned. This gift is distinct from the practice in some modern denominations where speaking in tongues is seen as an ecstatic, unintelligible speech. Instead, the biblical gift of tongues involves the miraculous capacity to communicate the gospel and other divine truths in foreign languages, enabling disciples to reach people groups they could not previously communicate with. This gift was prominently displayed on the day of Pentecost in Acts 2, where the apostles spoke in various languages understood by the diverse crowd gathered in Jerusalem, each hearing the message in their native tongue. This miraculous event served as a powerful witness to the presence and power of the Holy Spirit, breaking down language barriers and uniting people from different backgrounds in the truth of the gospel.

For disciples, the gift of speaking in tongues is a tool for evangelism and mission work, empowering them to share the gospel with individuals and communities that speak different languages. This gift not only facilitates communication but also serves as a sign of God's inclusive nature, showing that the message of Christ is for all nations and peoples. When used properly, speaking in tongues can bridge cultural and linguistic divides, allowing disciples to effectively minister in diverse contexts and fulfill the Great Commission to make disciples of all nations. It is important for disciples to recognize that this gift, like all spiritual gifts, is given for the purpose of edifying the church and advancing God's kingdom. It should be exercised with humility, wisdom, and a clear understanding of its biblical purpose, ensuring that it aligns with the Holy Spirit's intent to bring clarity and understanding, rather than confusion or division.

The Interpretation of Tongues: The gift of interpretation of tongues is a spiritual gift that enables disciples to understand and interpret languages that they have never studied or previously understood. This gift works in conjunction with the gift of speaking in tongues, allowing the message spoken in a foreign language to be comprehended and communicated to others who might not understand the original language. In the early church, this gift was vital during gatherings where someone might speak in tongues, as it ensured that the entire congregation could benefit from the message being delivered. The gift of interpretation is not about translating word-for-word but rather conveying the meaning and intent of what is spoken, ensuring that the message aligns with God's will and edifies the church.

For disciples, the gift of interpretation of tongues is essential for maintaining unity and clarity within the body of Christ, particularly in multicultural or multilingual contexts. This gift allows for the seamless sharing of God's word across language barriers, enabling the gospel to be understood by all present. It also prevents confusion and ensures that the supernatural act of speaking in tongues serves its intended purpose: to glorify God and build up the church. Disciples with this gift must exercise it with discernment, humility, and a deep reliance on the Holy Spirit to accurately convey the message. Like all spiritual gifts, the interpretation of tongues should be used to serve others, promote understanding, and advance the mission of the church in bringing the good news of Jesus Christ to all people, regardless of language or culture.

Additional Gifts:

In addition to the gifts listed in 1 Corinthians 12, Paul also mentions other important gifts in Romans 12:6-8, such as teaching, encouragement, giving, leadership, and mercy. These gifts, though not always classified under the same categories as those in 1 Corinthians 12, are equally significant in their contribution to the church's mission. Teaching equips the body with sound doctrine, encouragement provides comfort and motivation, giving supports the work of ministry, leadership guides the church, and mercy extends compassion and support to those in need. These gifts reflect the breadth of the Spirit's empowerment, showing that the Holy Spirit works through various means to foster growth, unity, and effectiveness in the church.

Paul emphasizes in 1 Corinthians 12:11 that the distribution of these gifts is solely at the discretion of the Holy Spirit: "All these are the work of one and the same Spirit, and he distributes them to each one, just as he determines." This underscores the principle that spiritual gifts are not acquired through personal effort or merit but are given according to God's sovereign will. No disciple can claim or earn a specific gift; rather, it is the Spirit who chooses how and to whom each gift is given. This reinforces the idea that spiritual gifts are meant to serve the collective needs of the church and advance God's purposes, not to elevate individuals or create divisions. The recognition of this divine sovereignty fosters humility and unity among disciples, encouraging them to use their gifts in service to one another and the broader mission of the church.

The Purpose of Spiritual Gifts

The primary purpose of spiritual gifts is to build up the church, the body of Christ. In Ephesians 4:12-13, Paul explains that the gifts are given "to equip his people for works of service, so that the body of Christ may be built up until we all reach unity in the faith and in the knowledge of the Son of God and become mature, attaining to the whole measure of the fullness of Christ." The gifts are intended to promote spiritual growth, encourage unity, and help the church achieve maturity in Christ.

Spiritual gifts also serve to glorify God and advance His kingdom. When disciples use their gifts faithfully, they are participating in God's work on earth, demonstrating His power and love to the world. The gifts are also a testimony to the presence of the Holy Spirit in the church, as they manifest His power in ways that go beyond human ability. For example, gifts of healing and miracles serve as signs that point to the reality of God's kingdom, while gifts of prophecy and wisdom provide guidance and insight that reveal God's will for His people.

In addition to building up the church and glorifying God, spiritual gifts also serve to meet the needs of the community. The gifts of giving, mercy, and help, for example, are often used to address the physical, emotional, and spiritual needs of others. When disciples use these gifts, they are extending God's love and compassion to those in need, reflecting the character of Christ in their actions.

The Proper Use and Potential Misuse of Spiritual Gifts

The proper use of spiritual gifts is guided by love and humility. In 1 Corinthians 13, Paul emphasizes that even the most extraordinary gifts are meaningless without love. He writes, "If I speak in the tongues of men or of angels, but do not have love, I am only a resounding gong or a clanging cymbal" (1 Corinthians 13:1). Love must be the motivation behind the use of any spiritual gift, as it ensures that the gift is used for the benefit of others and not for self-glorification. Additionally, humility is essential in using spiritual gifts, as it acknowledges that the gifts are given by God's grace and are not a result of personal merit or effort.

The misuse of spiritual gifts can occur when they are used for selfish purposes, to create division, or to elevate oneself above others. Paul addresses these issues in 1 Corinthians 12-14, where he provides guidelines for the orderly use of gifts in the church. He cautions against the overemphasis on certain gifts, such as speaking in tongues, which had become a source of pride and division in the Corinthian church. Paul reminds the disciples that all gifts are equally valuable and that the purpose of the gifts is to edify the church, not to exalt the individual.

Another potential misuse of spiritual gifts is neglecting to use them altogether. In the parable of the talents (Matthew 25:14-30), Jesus warns against burying one's gifts out of fear or laziness. Disciples are called to be faithful stewards of the gifts they have received, using them to serve others and advance God's kingdom. Failing to do so not only deprives the church of the benefits of those gifts but also dishonors the Giver, who entrusted the gifts to be used for His purposes.

Conclusion

The gifts of the Holy Spirit are a vital part of the life and ministry of the church. They are given by God to equip disciple s for service, to build up the body of Christ, and to glorify God in the world. When used properly, in love and humility, these gifts become powerful tools for advancing God's kingdom and meeting the needs of others. However, disciples must be vigilant against the misuse of these gifts, whether through selfishness, division, or neglect. By understanding the biblical basis, purpose, and proper use of spiritual gifts, the church can ensure that these gifts fulfill their intended role in God's plan for His people.

Chapter 11: The Role of the Holy Spirit in Prayer and Intercession

The Holy Spirit plays a pivotal role in the prayer life of a disciple, guiding, empowering, and interceding in ways that deepen and enrich the disciple 's communication with God. As the manifestation of God's will, the Holy Spirit is integral to the disciple 's prayer life, transforming it from a mere ritual to a profound and dynamic relationship with God. This chapter explores the multifaceted role of the Holy Spirit in prayer and intercession, highlighting how He assists, empowers, and intercedes on behalf of disciples.

Praying in the Spirit

Praying in the Spirit is a profound and transformative aspect of a disciple's prayer life, as emphasized in Ephesians 6:18: "And pray in the Spirit on all occasions with all kinds of prayers and requests." This form of prayer transcends mere verbal communication, engaging the Holy Spirit to guide and influence the disciple's prayer life. By praying in the Spirit, disciples invite the Holy Spirit to take an active role in their prayers, allowing Him to shape both the content and the direction of their petitions. This process involves a surrender to the Holy Spirit's leading, moving beyond personal desires and limitations to align with God's broader purposes and divine will.

When disciples pray in the Spirit, they experience a deepened connection with God, as the Holy Spirit helps to overcome the constraints of human language and understanding. The Spirit provides the words or groans needed to express prayers that might otherwise be difficult to articulate. This divine assistance ensures that prayers are not limited by the speaker's ability or knowledge but are infused with a higher understanding and alignment with God's intentions. This might manifest in various ways, including spontaneous expressions of worship, the use of spiritual languages (Hebrew), or a heightened sensitivity to God's leading, all of which reflect a deeper level of engagement with God's Spirit.

Furthermore, praying in the Spirit often leads to a more profound sense of spiritual connection and insight. The Holy Spirit can reveal aspects of

God's will and purposes that are beyond human comprehension, enabling disciple s to pray in alignment with divine intentions. This deeper level of prayer fosters a more intimate relationship with God, allowing for prayers that are both heartfelt and effective. By embracing this practice, disciples open themselves to the transformative power of the Holy Spirit, experiencing a prayer life that is enriched, empowered, and closely aligned with the heart of God.

Intercession

Intercession is a fundamental role of the Holy Spirit in the life of a disciple, as highlighted in Romans 8:26-27: "In the same way, the Spirit helps us in our weakness. We do not know what we ought to pray for, but the Spirit himself intercedes for us through wordless groans. And he who searches our hearts knows the mind of the Spirit, because the Spirit intercedes for God's people in accordance with the will of God." This passage reveals the Holy Spirit's crucial function in bridging the gap between human limitations and divine will. When disciples are uncertain or overwhelmed by their circumstances, the Spirit steps in to intercede on their behalf, expressing their needs and desires in a way that aligns perfectly with God's purposes. This divine intercession ensures that even when disciples are unsure of what to pray for, their prayers are still effective and meaningful.

The Spirit's intercession is characterized by its depth and intimacy. Through "wordless groans," the Holy Spirit articulates the inexpressible needs and burdens of the disciple 's heart, providing a profound connection between the human experience and divine intervention. This aspect of intercession reflects the Spirit's deep understanding of both the disciple 's inner struggles and the broader context of God's will. The Holy Spirit, who searches and knows the human heart, is uniquely positioned to offer prayers that are not only deeply personal but also perfectly aligned with God's plan. This ensures that every intercessory prayer is infused with divine wisdom and purpose, offering reassurance to disciple s that their prayers are being powerfully and accurately presented to God.

By facilitating this kind of intercession, the Holy Spirit provides disciples with a source of profound comfort and confidence in their prayer life. Knowing that the Spirit intercedes with perfect alignment to God's will allows disciple s to approach prayer with a sense of security and peace, even when they feel incapable of expressing their needs clearly. This divine assistance transforms the prayer process, making it less about human ability and more about the Spirit's active role in guiding and enhancing prayer. The result is a prayer life that is deeply enriched, profoundly effective, and intimately connected to the heart of God.

The Spirit's Help in Weakness and Uncertainty

In times of weakness or uncertainty, the role of the Holy Spirit in prayer becomes especially vital for disciples. Prayer can be particularly challenging when individuals face personal struggles, doubts, or emotional turmoil. During these moments, the Holy Spirit steps in to provide much-needed comfort and support, helping disciples to pray with genuine sincerity and perseverance. His presence alleviates the burden of feeling inadequate or lost in prayer, offering a divine anchor that stabilizes the disciple's prayer life. The Spirit's guidance ensures that even when prayers feel feeble or unclear, they are still directed towards God with integrity and purpose.

The Holy Spirit brings peace and clarity to a troubled prayer life, transforming confusion into focused, meaningful dialogue with God. When disciples are overwhelmed by their circumstances or uncertain of how to articulate their needs, the Holy Spirit works to clear the fog of anxiety and doubt. This divine intervention enables disciple s to approach prayer with renewed clarity and intention, helping them to navigate through emotional and spiritual struggles. The Spirit's influence helps refine and direct prayers, ensuring that they align with God's will and purpose, even when the disciple's own understanding is limited.

By relying on the Holy Spirit in times of difficulty, disciples experience a profound sense of connection with God, knowing that their prayers are guided and supported beyond their own capabilities. This reliance transforms prayer from a solitary struggle into a collaborative process with the Spirit, who intercedes with divine insight and strength. This partnership in prayer not only empowers disciples to persist through their challenges but also reassures them that their spiritual efforts are both heard and effective. In essence, the Holy Spirit's role in these times of weakness provides a deeper, more intimate experience of God's presence and guidance, enriching the disciple's prayer life and strengthening their faith.

Conclusion

In conclusion, the Holy Spirit's involvement in prayer and intercession is both transformative and essential for the disciple 's spiritual growth and effectiveness. Through praying in the Spirit, interceding on behalf of disciples, and offering support in times of weakness, the Holy Spirit ensures that prayer remains a vital and dynamic part of the disciple's life. Embracing the Holy Spirit's role in prayer allows disciple s to experience deeper intimacy with God, greater alignment with His will, and a more profound impact in their intercessory efforts.

Chapter 12: Walking in the Spirit

Walking in the Spirit is a call to live in continuous alignment with the guidance and influence of the Holy Spirit in every aspect of life. For disciples, this means allowing the Holy Spirit to shape their thoughts, actions, and interactions in ways that reflect Christ's love and righteousness. This chapter offers practical advice and biblical wisdom on how to navigate everyday issues—such as decision-making, relationships, work, and worship—by walking in the Spirit.

Decision-Making

Decision-making is a crucial area where walking in the Spirit can significantly influence a disciple's life. The Holy Spirit serves as a divine guide, offering wisdom and discernment that helps disciples make choices aligned with God's will and purposes. This guidance is not always immediate or obvious but requires an active engagement in seeking the Spirit's counsel. Disciples are encouraged to approach decisions with a mindset of prayerful reflection, asking the Holy Spirit for clarity and insight. James 1:5 assures disciples that if they lack wisdom, they can ask God, who gives liberally. The Holy Spirit, as the embodiment of divine wisdom, plays an integral role in this process, providing the necessary insight to make decisions that honor God and reflect His intentions.

In practical terms, seeking the Spirit's guidance involves a combination of prayer, studying Scripture, and being attentive to the Spirit's promptings. Prayer serves as a direct line of communication with God, allowing disciples to present their concerns and decisions before Him. Studying Scripture provides a foundation of God's principles and teachings, which can illuminate the path forward. The Holy Spirit often speaks through the still, small voice within, through a sense of peace or unease, or through the counsel of fellow disciples. By integrating these elements into the decision-making process, disciples can ensure that their choices are not merely driven by personal preferences or circumstances but are aligned with God's broader plans.

Cultivating sensitivity to the Spirit's voice is essential for effective decision-making. This involves being open and responsive to guidance that may sometimes challenge personal desires or require steps of faith. It is important for disciples to remain humble and flexible, acknowledging that God's ways are higher than human ways. This openness allows the Holy Spirit to direct their decisions in ways that may surpass their own understanding but ultimately lead to greater fulfillment and alignment with God's will. By embracing the Spirit's guidance, disciples can navigate life's choices with confidence, knowing that their decisions are grounded in divine wisdom and purpose.

Relationships

The Holy Spirit plays a crucial role in shaping and guiding relationships, fostering the development of key virtues essential for healthy and Christ-centered interactions. Galatians 5:22-23 outlines the fruit of the Spirit, which includes love, patience, kindness, and self-control. These attributes are fundamental for nurturing meaningful relationships and embodying Christ's teachings. When disciples walk in the Spirit, these qualities become evident in their daily interactions, allowing them to build connections that reflect God's love and grace. The Spirit's influence helps believers approach relationships with a heart of compassion and understanding, creating an environment where positive, Christ-centered relationships can flourish.

In navigating interpersonal conflicts, the Holy Spirit provides the wisdom and strength needed to respond with grace and forgiveness. The Spirit empowers disciples to handle disagreements without escalating tensions, offering solutions that promote reconciliation and mutual respect. Practical steps, such as actively listening to others and practicing empathy, are essential in this process. By seeking the Spirit's guidance, disciples can respond to conflicts in ways that honor God and reflect His love, ensuring that even challenging interactions contribute to the growth and health of the relationship. This approach helps maintain a spirit of unity and peace, which is vital for fostering long-lasting, Christ-centered connections.

Furthermore, the Holy Spirit assists disciples in choosing relationships that support their spiritual growth and align with God's will. This involves discerning which relationships are nurturing and which might be detrimental to one's faith journey. By relying on the Spirit's guidance, believers can make choices that enhance their spiritual well-being and contribute to their overall growth in Christ. The Holy Spirit provides insight into the dynamics of relationships and helps disciples form connections that are spiritually enriching and supportive of their walk with God. This divine guidance ensures that relationships are not only fulfilling on a personal level but also contribute positively to one's spiritual journey and alignment with God's purpose.

Work and Worship

In the realms of work and worship, walking in the Spirit profoundly impacts how disciples approach their daily tasks and spiritual practices. In the workplace, the Holy Spirit provides guidance for disciples to approach their responsibilities with integrity, diligence, and excellence. Colossians 3:23 encourages believers to "And whatsoever ye do, do *it* heartily, as to the Lord, and not unto men" This perspective transforms everyday tasks into opportunities to serve God and reflect His character. The Spirit helps disciples see their work as an extension of their faith, motivating them to perform their duties with a sense of purpose and devotion that honors God and serves as a witness to His goodness.

Similarly, the influence of the Holy Spirit extends to worship, where He leads disciples into deeper and more authentic expressions of praise and reverence. True worship is not confined to specific times or places but permeates every aspect of a disciple's life. The Holy Spirit helps believers cultivate a heart of worship that remains engaged with God throughout their daily routines. This involves allowing the Spirit to guide their expressions of praise, whether in structured worship services or in everyday moments of gratitude and reflection. By walking in the Spirit, disciples can experience a richer and more profound connection with God, integrating worship into all areas of their lives and reflecting their faith through their actions and attitudes.

The Spirit's role in work and worship underscores the holistic nature of living a Spirit-led life. In work, the Spirit transforms mundane tasks into acts of worship and service, ensuring that disciples approach their roles with a mindset that honors God and impacts others positively. In worship, the Holy Spirit deepens the disciple's experience of God, enabling them to worship with sincerity and joy in every aspect of life. By walking in the Spirit, disciples allow their faith to influence not only their spiritual practices but also their daily endeavors, creating a seamless integration of their spiritual and practical lives that reflects the fullness of their relationship with God.

In summary, walking in the Spirit offers a practical and transformative approach to daily living. By seeking the Spirit's guidance in decision-making, nurturing relationships, and approaching work and worship with a Spirit-led mindset, disciples can experience a more vibrant and effective Disciple life. The Holy Spirit's influence provides wisdom, empowers disciples to embody Christ's love, and infuses daily activities with divine purpose, making the journey of faith both purposeful and deeply connected to God's will.

About the Author

Karajah Yashar is a dedicated scholar and disciple of Christ with a deep commitment to sharing God's wisdom through his work. A graduate of Rutgers University, Karajah has built a diverse career working with notable institutions including Rutgers University, the University of Central Florida, and The Transition House. His professional experiences encompass counseling incarcerated men, teaching both youth and adults, and supporting the homeless population, reflecting his profound dedication to serving those in need.

In 2016, Karajah founded Black Scripture Press, an Orlando-based publishing house with a mission to disseminate God's wisdom and teachings. This endeavor highlights his passion for spreading the word of God and providing resources that inspire and educate believers. Karajah's journey of faith began with his rebirth and baptism in the Holy Spirit in 2001, a transformative experience that has since shaped his life's work and dedication to the study and writing of Scripture.

With a focus on integrating faith into practical living, Karajah Yashar continues to contribute to the church community through his writings and publishing efforts. His work embodies a lifelong commitment to exploring and sharing the depths of God's word, aiming to encourage and equip disciples to walk in the Spirit and live out their faith with conviction and purpose.

www.ingramcontent.com/pod-product-compliance
Lightning Source LLC
Chambersburg PA
CBHW071012120626
46546CB00003B/1052